# NATIVE GENIUS IN ANONYMOUS ARCHITECTURE

NORTH GABLE, HENRY WHITFIELD STONE HOUSE, GUILFORD, CONNECTICUT, 1639

# NATIVE GENIUS

HORIZON PRESS INC   *New York*   1957

# IN ANONYMOUS

# ARCHITECTURE

## BY SIBYL MOHOLY-NAGY

# WITH HOMAGE TO FRANK LLOYD WRIGHT    *who wrote in 1910:*

*The true basis for any serious study of the art of Architecture still lies in those indigenous, more humble buildings everywhere that are to architecture what folklore is to literature or folk song to music and with which academic architects were seldom concerned . . . These many folk structures are of the soil, natural. Though often slight, their virtue is intimately related to environment and to the heart-life of the people. Functions are usually truthfully conceived and rendered invariably with natural feeling. Results are often beautiful and always instructive.*    —*from* THE SOVEREIGNTY OF THE INDIVIDUAL

# CONTENTS

*Page* 17   PART ONE
NATIVE GENIUS IN ANONYMOUS ARCHITECTURE

49   PART TWO
SITE AND CLIMATE

| | |
|---|---|
| Landscape | 58 |
| The Inclusive Site | 64 |
| The Exclusive Site | 66 |
| The Defensive Site | 68 |
| The Working Site | 74 |
| The City Site | 78 |
| Climate | 83 |
| Cold | 84 |
| Snow | 86 |
| Heat | 92 |
| Rain | 98 |

105   PART THREE
FORM AND FUNCTION

| | |
|---|---|
| The Dwelling | 114 |
| Working Space | 128 |

|  |  | Storage | 142 |
|  |  | Defense | 147 |
|  |  | Worship | 155 |
| 167 | PART FOUR |  |  |
|  | MATERIALS AND SKILLS | Stone | 176 |
|  |  | Brick | 182 |
|  |  | Wood | 188 |
|  |  | Adobe | 196 |
|  |  | Fibre | 202 |
| 205 | PART FIVE |  |  |
|  | A SENSE OF QUALITY | The Roof | 209 |
|  |  | The Corner | 212 |
|  |  | The Base | 214 |
|  |  | Access | 216 |
|  |  | AUTHOR'S NOTE | 221 |
|  |  | CREDITS | 223 |

# ILLUSTRATIONS

Frontispiece: Henry Whitfield Stone House, Guilford, Connecticut

Plate 1   Cloisters of San Lorenzo, Florence, Italy   *page 21*

2   Reconstructed Neolithic Lake Dwelling, Lake Constance, Germany   *26*

3   Diagrammatic Section of an Italian Trulli and an Irish Cairn   *28*

4   Stein-am-Rhein, Switzerland   *30*

5   Cactus Hut, Otomi Region, Hidalgo, Mexico   *31*

6   Winery, Russian Colony, Sonomo County, California   *32*

7   Carved Corner Column, Chiapas, Mexico   *34*

8   Mexican Village Well   *35*

9   Real Estate Development, New York State   *37*

10   Levittown Speculation House; and Abraham Hasbrook House, New Paltz, New York   *39*

11   Dymaxion House by Buckminster Fuller, Erected in North Carolina, 1940   *41*

12   Street in Cap Haitien, Haiti   *43*

13   Wall Decorations in Mittenwald, Germany   *45*

14   16th Century Inn, Switzerland   *46*

15  Church at Trampas, New Mexico   *47*

16  Mansion, Auburn, New York, 1813   *54*

17  Windows, "Place of the Hummingbird," Huitziltepec, Mexico, 17th Century   *56*

18  Diagram, Andalusian Window   *57*

19  Hacienda near Puebla, Mexico   *58*

20  Village Piazza, Costillo, New Mexico   *60*

21  Court of an Old Grange near La Malabie, Quebec, Canada   *63*

22  Farm in the Foot Hills of the Diablo Range, California   *65*

23  Church at Wounded Knee, South Dakota   *66*

24  Diagram, Aerial View of Fortress *La Ferière*, Haiti   *68*

25  Fortress *La Ferière*, Haiti   *69*

26  The Cloisters, Ephrata, Pennsylvania   *70*

27  Diagram, Old Hospital, Strasbourg, France   *72*

28  Diagram, "Quarter-Sawn" Log   *72*

29  Dormer Roof, The Cloisters, Ephrata, Pennsylvania   *73*

30  Diagram, Section Through Sugar Cane Mill   *74*

31  Sugar Cane Mill, Buccaneer Plantation, St. Croix, Virgin Islands   *75*

32  Dutch Grist Mill, Hudson Valley, New York   *77*

33  Rhinelander Gardens, New York   *79*

34  Coal Mining Town Tenement, Boone County, West Virginia   *81*

35  Lumberman's Cabin, Bald Mountain Range, Colorado   *85*

36  Old Powder Storage House, Ouray, Colorado   *86*

37  Diagram, Section Through a Norwegian Stave Church   *88*

38  Cotton Mill, Vermont   *89*

39  Two Barns on the Reservation of Fort Klamath, Oregon   *91*

40  House Built by a Retired Sea Captain, St. Croix, Virgin Islands   *93*

41  House of a Banana Field Worker, Vera Cruz Region, Mexico   *94*

42   Mountain Caille, Range de Marmelade, Haiti   *97*

43   Diagrammatic Presentation of Air Currents in Plate 44   *96*

44   Haitian Peasant House in the Valley   *97*

45   Diagrammatic Presentation of Inside Thatch of Plate 46   *98*

46   Jacal or Straw House, Puebla, Mexico   *99*

47   Diagrammatic Presentation of Roof Overhang and of Building Arrangement in Plate 48   *100*

48   Street in Pichucalco, Chiapas, Mexico   *101*

49   Overhang, Main Street of Huatchinango, Vera Cruz, Mexico   *103*

50   Possum Run Cabin, Alabama   *108*

51   Chinese Incense Burner and Greek Hydra   *109*

52   New England Saltbox, Connecticut   *112*

53   Plans of Glamis Castle and Henry Whitfield House   *114*

54   Henry Whitfield Stone House, Guilford, Connecticut, 1639   *115*

55   Chimney Detail, Whitfield House   *117*

56   First Philipse Manor House, North Tarrytown, New York   *119*

57   Town House, Cap Haitien, Haiti   *121*

58   Typical Street in Port-au-Prince, Haiti   *122*

59   Acona Pueblo, New Mexico   *125*

60   House of the Territorial Period, California   *125*

61   Diagram of Wood Circe   *126*

62   Stone House, Otomi Region, Hidalgo, Mexico   *127*

63   Stone House, Close-up of Gable End   *127*

64   Kitchen Hut, El Tule, Oaxaca, Mexico   *128*

65   "Folded" Gable, Überlingen, Germany   *130*

66   Barn near Estherville, Iowa   *131*

67   Diagram of Barn Construction   *134*

68   Overhang Houses, Germany   *133*

69   Mennonite Barn, Lancaster County, Pennsylvania   *135*

70   Circular Stone Barn, New Lebanon, New York   *137*

71   Circular Barn, Clinton, Pennsylvania   *139*

72   Village Well, Christiansted, St. Croix, Virgin Islands   *140*

73   Penobscot Indian Bark Hut   *142*

74   Storage Bins, now Farmhand Houses, Zacatecas, Mexico   *143*

75   Granary, Valley of Oaxaca, Mexico   *144*

76   Corn Crib, New Hampshire   *145*

77   Fortified Granary, Probably 17th Century, Teotyucan, Mexico   *148*

78   *El Rollo*, Tepeaca, Puebla, Mexico   *149*

79   Diagram, Fort Edgecomb Construction   *150*

80   Fort Edgecomb, Maine, 1808   *151*

81   Interior, Fortress *La Ferière*, Haiti   *153*

82   Diagram, Moorish Embroidery and Ceiling Decoration, Ilita   *156*

83   Fortified Village Church, Ilita, Puebla, Mexico   *157*

84   Franciscan Church, Xochimilco, Mexico   *159*

85   Diagram of One Gable at Christianborg Palace, Copenhagen, Denmark   *160*

86   Chapel, Armstrong Plantation, St. Croix, Virgin Islands   *161*

87   Presbyterian Church and Parsonage, New Milford, Connecticut   *163*

88   Tombs in a Cemetery near Port-au-Prince, Haiti   *165*

89   Painted Barn Front, Ile d'Orléans, Quebec, Canada   *170*

90   Corner of Well House, New Hope, Pennsylvania   *172*

91   Corner of Huguenot House, New Paltz, New York   *172*

92   Corner of Medieval Half-timber House   *173*

93   Ohio River Inn, Late 18th Century   *174*

94   Wall of a Ruined Hacienda near San Udefonso Hueyotlipan, Mexico   *177*

95   Wall detail of an Octagonal Cobblestone House, Madison, New York   *177*

96   Double House, New Hope, Pennsylvania   *179*

97   Wine Storehouse, St. Thomas, Virgin Islands   *180*

98   Wine Storehouse, St. Thomas, Virgin Islands   *181*

99   South Wall of a Brick Barn, Lancaster County, Pennsylvania   *183*

100   Dutch Oven, Senate House, Kingston-on-Hudson, New York   *183*

101   Entrance to a Patio, El Tepeaca, Puebla, Mexico   *184*

102   Detail from the Casa de Alfenique, Puebla, Mexico   *185*

103   Entrance to Slave Quarters, Abandoned Sugar Plantation, Jamaica   *186*

104   Close-up of Hall of the Cloisters, Ephrata, Pennsylvania   *189*

105   Diagram, False Gable of Lombard Church   *190*

106   Abandoned Wholesale Store, Bay City, Michigan   *191*

107   Close-up of Shingles, Wyckoff House, Brooklyn, New York   *192*

108   Drawing of Carpathian Mountain Chapel   *192*

109   Grist Mill, Long Island, New York   *193*

110   Log House, New Mexico   *195*

111   Lumberjack Cabin near Jonquière, Quebec, Canada   *195*

112   Diagram of Terrone Brick   *196*

113   Viga Ceiling   *198*

114   Church at Trampas, New Mexico   *199*

115   Village Well, Libres, Mexico   *199*

116   Baking Stoves and North Buildings, Taos, New Mexico   *200*

117   Summer Bower around Haitian House   *202*

118   Granja Linda near Tulancingo, Hidalgo, Mexico   *209*

119   Diagram, Construction of Thatched Roof in Plate 120   *210*

120   Mestizzo House, Maya Region, Chiapas, Mexico   *211*

121   House in Cajon Construction of a Navajo Shepherd, Arizona   *212*

122 Wood Quoins of a Tenant House, Mohawk Valley, New York 1887 *213*

123 The Wilson Popenoe House, Antigua, Guatemala *214*

124 Circular Manor of Abandoned Plantation near Christiansted, St. Croix, Virgin Islands *215*

125 Divided Dutch Door, Van Deusen House, Hurley, New York, 1723 *216*

126 Gate in the Abode Wall of the Old Town, Albuquerque, New Mexico *218*

# NATIVE GENIUS IN ANONYMOUS ARCHITECTURE *part one*

# NATIVE GENIUS IN ANONYMOUS ARCHITECTURE

Buildings are transmitters of life. They transmit the life of the past into the lives of the future—if they are more than mere shelter and more than borrowed form. A people without architecture transmits little of its culture. Each phase of its history ends with the death of the generation that created it. The narrow realm of Justinian's Byzantine state, for instance, became the cultural link between Antiquity and Medieval Europe through its architecture, while the vast empire of Alaric, the Goth, standing at the same threshold of history, is no more than a dim legend. Forgotten is Suleiman the Magnificent, while his much weaker contemporary, Francis I, survives as the style-giver of the French Renaissance. The lack of architectural self-expression of many great peoples terminated their day in history beyond recall. A culture then asserts its place in the annals of mankind most forcefully through the acknowledged contribution its leaders made to architecture: classified, catalogued, and evaluated by scholars with platonical detachment from its contemporary function. But beyond this pedigreed "history in stone" exists an architecture that transmits a different aspect of life. It testifies to the aspirations of the group. Its buildings tell not the official but the private history of a culture—the unending struggle for physical and spiritual survival of anonymous men. Indigenous buildings speak the vernacular of the people.

In an age that has become myopic from gazing at the stupendous proportions of its technological structures, Americans are blind to the wealth of anonymous buildings in their own hemisphere. A traditional inferiority complex searches for architectural significance, even in Folk Architecture, in Asia and Europe rather than close to home. A Cottswold cottage or a Japanese Shoin house seems more interesting and instructive than a woven Indian hut or Pennsylvania-Dutch stone work. The romantic glow of the ancient and the far-away has dimmed for us the achievements of our own untutored and intuitive architectural geniuses. Their names are unknown and their work unclassified. It is this very anonymity that gives special weight to their work because it was preserved for no other reason than its adequacy beyond the life of the builder. It fulfilled an *ideal standard*.

Our own highly complicated way of life has produced architectural standards based on different values than those of pre-industrial times. These standards are concerned less and less with design and more and more with technology. Artificial needs, pitched by promotion, have obscured the fact that there is no progress in architecture, only progress in mechanical equipment. The Industrial Revolution has greatly improved man's physical environment. It is more comfortable to live in an air-conditioned apartment than in a pit-house, and more hygienic to use a toilet than a privy; but architecture, as the realization of man's search for anchorage in the current of time, is non-progressive. It develops not in a graphic curve but in cycles, as do all things of the mind and the heart. The "utility core" of a contemporary glass house that invades the living room with kitchen activities, or the thirty-story dwelling hive that invades the privacy of marriage with the noises of other lives, would have seemed as regressive to a Renaissance family as a Piano Nobile or a Minstrel Gallery seems to a modern family.

An architectural cycle has reached its high point when the architect has fulfilled the causal needs and aspirations of his own times in a design that is serviceable and timelessly beautiful (Plate 1). These might seem big words, applicable only to historical buildings of acknowledged fame. Yet the best among anonymous buildings in the

1. CLOISTERS OF SAN LORENZO, FLORENCE, ITALY

New World carry the same message. They are triumphant statements of architectural service and architectural significance. They are transmitters of life (Frontispiece).

But the value of vernacular architecture goes deeper than these qualities of adequate expression which it shares with pre-designed academic buildings. In addition to service and esthetic appeal, the structures built by settlers in a new land can serve as visual means to come closer to an understanding of the causes of architecture. They are in the actual meaning of the term primitive, meaning not simple but *original*. This concern with the original roots of architecture has been attacked as a romantic evasion of contemporary building problems. The fact remains, however, that the basic task of the builder, the task which distinguishes him from the engineer and the contractor, is still the sheltering of man, his work and his possessions in structures that provide spiritual as well as material gratifications.

The architect of today has a hard time holding on to this mission. He is challenged and confused at every turn by technology, economy, and a waning commitment of the public to cultural and esthetic values. There was a time when houses were built by unchallenged and unconfused architects whose ambition was total service to man. To look at their solutions might provide a much-needed inspiration without which no creative work, large or small, is possible. It might confirm the beleaguered architect in his calling as the artificer of form and space for the sheltering of body and soul. The academies are closed. The great unifying ideas of homogeneous societies no longer supply a natural common denominator. The architect of today is on his own. His search for a re-definition of his role between function and expression must focus on technology *and* the human equation. Wotton, some 300 years ago, spoke of the architect as "a diver into causes." It is he and no one else who must justify serviceable structure through the architectural idea. And this idea, this *first cause of architecture as shelter*, was and is the separation of human environment from natural environment.

Separation from nature has become easy enough. Natural forces are countered by technological forces, from earth-moving equipment to air conditioning, but the first cause of domestic architecture is still the same. Rampant natural environment as the perpetual threat to man's self-willed order has been replaced by industrial environment which threatens the matrix of human life with the same forces of chaos and extinction as did jungle, sea, sky and volcano. To provide *the home as an ideal standard* is still the architect's first cause, no matter how great and rewarding are his other contributions to monumental and technological building. The delineation of the place where man can grow, in spite of the dehumanizing forces of mechanization and de-personalization, must be the concern of the architect. He has to fight for it with the same fierce determination with which the land settler cleared his place to live in the wilderness. As those builders of old, the architect of today has to create *an anonymous architecture for the anonymous men* of the Industrial Age. Without new environmental standards provided by architecture the anonymous multitude will be unable to retain an at-homeness on this factory-strewn earth, and its morale will be broken.

What then is a man-made environment? The term environment itself is ambiguous, having lost its proper identity and serving all definitions with impartial imprecision. As victims of perpetual self-analysis, we have become used to speaking quite meaninglessly of conscious and subconscious environment, of environments economical, political, collective, individual, creative, oppressive, controlled, religious, and a dozen others. But the root of the word "environment" is quite simple: "to veer around," to define by circumambulation that much of the earth's surface as lies within reach of individual man. The only "environmental responses" our pre-analytical forebears knew were provided by the actual physical space they lived in "as the logical condition for the existence of bodies" as Euclid put it. In this primordial space *homo sapiens* had no more rights than any other animal. He was organism among organisms in the unending cycle of conception, growth and death, weaker than most of his fellow animals, without fur and feather and the cyclical instinct of hibernation. He could not make himself invisible like the snow hare, nor secure his offspring in a pouch while foraging for food, nor loosen barbed quills from his back for defense. He needed shelter to protect his warm-blooded offspring and maintain the one posesssion no other animal had: FIRE. Perhaps it was this flame that lighted his evolutionary way. It kept him awake and scheming while the contented creatures slept. The possession of thermal energy outside his body metabolism was possibly the stimulus that separated the worst-equipped primate from the undistinguished generic mass. He started to develop in himself that which was specific. Dimly he anticipated himself as an individual, and his gains as lasting instead of as merely sustaining. No achievements in the milleniums to come would ever match the magnitude of this development toward a man-made social environment.

Nature, it has been said, abhors a vacuum, but she abhors even more the three concepts on which hinged the genesis of the architectural evolution: *economy, diversity,* and *permanence.* Economy is alien to Nature. She is a wasteful progenitress. The continuation of life is guaranteed by sheer over-production. New matter crowds upon decay in wanton abundance. Only the maintenance of human life is based on economy, the first premise of which is the organization and upkeep of planned resources.

There is no diversity in the natural group. Every organism in its natural state is species, subject to generic law. Nothing is singular phenomenon. Exceptionality if it occurs is not exempt from cyclical laws; for on the lower levels of social intelligence the herd destroys the non-typical specimen. The human being, in contrast, gradually came to acknowledge non-uniformity within the laws of the group. Just as no two human skeletons are exactly identical, so each shelter, no matter how primitive, expresses in some detail a specific, non-collective need.

But it was the claim to permanence that flung the boldest challenge at natural law. The first Paleolithic man who rubbed two stones together to produce fire, instead of waiting for the accidental provision by lightning or spontaneous combustion, took on Nature as an antagonist. The first builder who constructed for himself a more durable protection than the vulnerable skin provided by an improvident Nature, opened the contest between the staying power of man and the transience of organic matter. In the most literal sense, he dug in to defend his claim. He could not liquidate death, but he added to the three material dimensions of building the fourth dimension of duration in time. Through the house he built he was assured a spiritual survival in his group that surpassed his meagre physical life span. Like two streams, the continuity of birth and decay in nature, and the continuity of human aspiration run side by side through history.

We don't know when and why the knock-kneed pit dweller straightened himself, observed and evaluated his habitat and either decided to stay and transform what he possessed, or to migrate. The herders and farmers of the Neolithicum made another decisive step in the genesis of architecture. Instead of submitting to an *intrinsic* environment, they adapted a *selective* environment to human needs. Where the primordial surroundings proved unsuitable for human control, tribes set out in search of adaptable conditions. The appearance of the Semites in Mesopotamia, the Indo-Europeans in India and Greece, the Mongols in America, are a few examples of the drive toward a selective environment.

The ability of the settler to construct a complex and lasting shelter on alien ground was based on a proficiency, denied to the beast, and uniquely human; man could turn natural obstacles into assets. Alpine settlers built on the very surface of the glacial lakes (Plate 2). Mesopotamians transformed such unlikely building materials as river mud, reed and pitch into Ziggurats. The Eskimo survived by the very substance—snow—that should have defeated him biologically. With infinite humility the Neolithic settler adjusted himself to his selected environment, and with infinite cunning he imposed on it the concepts of man. Like a lover who delights in the discovery of more beauty in his love, he sought out the best features of location, material, and

2. RECONSTRUCTED NEOLITHIC LAKE DWELLING, LAKE CONSTANCE, GERMANY

climate to serve his purpose. Each designed structure in a selected and adapted environment separates once and for all that which is human from that which is natural. It was from this premise of purpose versus chaos that the architecture of man received its logic.

More decisive than this material progress was the growing self-consciousness of man, an awareness that he had endured through the pre-eminence of his brain. By evaluating his place in the creative scheme, he became conscious of his own measure and the magnitude of his achievement. It was this recognition of himself as a carrier of ultimate purpose that scaled down the gigantic images of the cave paintings to the realistic proportions of the New Stone Age. At the same point in history at which the settler gained control over nature he also gained control over the dual spheres of physical and spiritual forces. With this control starts the actual history of architecture as being predominantly *a selection of means and meanings in deliberately planned environments.* The confinement of the potent spirit to a place of worship would have seemed a futile undertaking to the Old Stone Age man. In his pre-artistic world everything at all times could contain the Real Presence, but man the settler learned to distinguish between purposes. To the divine spirit which in the magic-animistic past had favored the beast over the cave dweller, he now gave human characteristics. The settler separated his environments. The spiritual forces were relegated to the sacred district while in his earthly habitat he himself exercised control. Gradually he learned to think in three environmental dimensions—natural, human, and divine—and he never confused one with another.

The common people of Assyria left the winged monsters, the imported cedar logs and the multicolored terra cotta bricks to the sacred dwellings of their divine rulers. They constructed habitable space from the very earth on which they stood. Even a Boeotian peasant knew a temple when he saw one. The columned portico on a nineteenth century country house would have seemed to him as nonsensical and presumptuous as if he had been asked to plow his field in the ceremonial garb of a priest. From nature the land cultivator expected the

27

3. DIAGRAMMATIC SECTION OF AN ITALIAN
   TRULLI AND AN IRISH CAIRN

raw materials of shelter and sustenance; from his house he expected fitness and identification with the self and the group; from his temple he expected divine protection for his unending contest with nature. All three were essential parts of a planned environment that was man's only guarantee against chaos, the antithesis of human effort.

These then were the basic causes for the development of architecture: Diversity of form and function; economy of resources and up-keep; duration as material value and spiritual symbol. These causes created the anonymous architecture of Europe. The corbelled Trulli of Southern Italy, for instance, and the corbelled Cairns of Ireland, show closely related responses to given environmental conditions (Plate 3); but in addition to similarities, there are essential differences, based on specific circumstances. The Mediterranean climate demanded a heat-reflecting whitewash that is missing in the fog-bound North where an overgrowth of turf and shrub gives additional cold protection. The ancient building history of the South furnished the skill to construct a double-layered wall while the primitive North achieved only a single corbelled dome of dry-set stone. It is flared in the middle to gain stability which in Italy is assured through mortar and stucco.

The embattled peasant cultures of Europe were gradually forced to equalize their mode of living and building. The dire necessity of organized defense and mutual aid all but wiped out the open land settlement. The closed agricultural community, subservient to a protective overlord and a fixed spiritual dogma, became the predominant form of existence (Plate 4). The spontaneous response of the anonymous builder to the environmental challenge ceased. He submitted to *tradition* as the perpetuation of collective principles, regardless of their contemporary value.

This tyranny of traditional ideas was to a great extent cast off by the migrants who left Europe for the New World. They carried with them no desire to perpetuate traditions which had failed to provide the good life. Their most valuable import was *brauch*. This is a German word which can be translated approximately with the English words "usage" and "observance." In connection with building it signifies the

memory of the best past performance applied to new environmental demands. While the immigrants who founded the cities of the New World based their architecture mostly on the perpetuation of traditional ideas, and so created—at least in their official buildings—a nightmare of eclectic vulgarity, the land-takers planned their human and vegetative resources with the same care and cunning as their Neolithic ancestors. They staked the security of a limited environs and traditional observance on a tentative promise of prosperity and expansion. It was only by self-confidence in their selective judgment of new environment and old *brauch* that they could hope to survive. The heaped stone ring, a daubed wattle screen around a fire pit, or palisades of undressed timber or cacti (Plate 5), serving the earliest immigrants in their semi-nomadic existence, differed yet little from the nest, the hive and the burrow of the beast. It was a specifically human intelligence which did not limit itself to gravity and climate but created architecture by modifying that which is inherited and transforming that which is given.

5. CACTUS HUT, OTOMI REGION, HIDALGO, MEXICO

6. WINERY, RUSSIAN COLONY, SONOMO COUNTY, CALIFORNIA

32

A Russian wine grower in Sonomo County, California (Plate 6), for instance, who had followed the wagon train of Russian occupation in the early 19th century, combined the *brauch* of his origin with the demands of his new profession. He built his *ferma* in paled timber construction, customary throughout Russia. His gate towers have the octagonal "tent roof" of the Kremlin's Trinity Tower or the church at Kolomenskoe, correct to the brass spike, commemorating the tent pole, but here serving as lightning rod. The peculiar flat arch with dentil ends goes back to 1160 and the Bogoliubski Palace, but is eminently suitable here to admit team and wagon. It is built on the principle of the barrel maker's craft in bent wood construction, as are the towers with hoops of wine casks and slim uprights that are actually barrel staves.

The tension between the mechanical and climatic forces lined up against man, and the selected materials and skills countering this natural resistance, gives to anonymous buildings their beauty and their strength. A structure stands because man wills it so in spite of its mass that tends to fall. All architecture is, of course, so conceived. All material is subject to the forces of gravity and is upheld by human construction; and all walls provide climatic protection. But the chief claim of building technology is its theoretical universality. Calculation and scientific climatology have made building construction independent of architectural design. The behavior of a concrete wall is no longer the concern of the man who pours it, and any desired climate can be produced within four prefabricated walls anywhere on earth. In settler houses, on the other hand, every foot of ground, every stone, brick or piece of timber, every proportion, opening and wall angle is coordinated to answer to particular, never quite duplicated, challenges of site and gravity, of climate and human comfort.

Spontaneous building cannot be separated with a precise dividing line from technological and academic design. Simplified academic and technological elements do occur in anonymous architecture. They usually are an afterthought of a younger generation, moving gradually out of the settler pattern into an urban way of thinking, demonstrated

33

here in Plate 7. A carved corner column, echo of the baroque church in town, has been attached to a rubble and daub house in Chiapas, Mexico. Other concessions are those made to improved methods of husbandry as the wire cable on a Mexican village well that has replaced the ancient sisal rope (Plate 8).

7.   CARVED CORNER COLUMN, CHIAPAS, MEXICO

8.  MEXICAN VILLAGE WELL

"The group," wrote Henri Bergson, "must not be defined by the possession of certain characteristics but by the tendency to emphasize them." It is this special emphasis, the *leitmotif* of diversity, economy and permanence, that relates settler architecture from one rim of this continent to the other. Its hundred variations tell the story of conquering the natural chaos of a new world.

This folklore of building will be meaningless to those who define architecture either as pure esthetics, expressed in Le Corbusier's poetic exclamation: "Architecture is the play of light—supreme and magnificent—on significant form"; or to those who consider it predominantly a branch of modern technology, believing that "engineering will absorb architecture"[1] and that the architect's function can only be defined in the turgid phraseology of the technocrat: "catalyzing cooperative and potential resources into realigned and realizable technology and management strategy, providing demonstrable increase in performance increments per units of invested resources."[2]

Between these two extremes there is a growing awareness that architecture is neither the sophisticated libertinism of the artist who is responsible only to his own genius, nor the simple-minded mechanical objectivity of the slide rule, no matter how scientifically disguised. The variety of problems, inherent today in the architectural task, makes it more than ever a selective and coordinative function. It is a challenge of responsible choices with the ultimate aim of total *coherence*. A good vernacular structure, being eminently selective, coordinative and coherent, is of similar architectural importance.

This importance is insignificant compared to the gigantic building projects of industry and communities. Factories, office skyscrapers, mammoth schools and hospitals dominate the architectural scene. Yet, vast numbers of our population depend for their happiness on the qualities that make non-urban buildings good architecture. Our big cities are exploding rapidly. From Maine to San Diego, "developments"

[1] J. Hudnut, "The Engineer's Esthetics." (Architectural Record, January 1956).
[2] Buckminster Fuller, "Considerations for an Architectural Curriculum." (Student Publication of the North Carolina State College, October 1954).

36

are crawling along the highways, depositing along their destructive trail an unending string of inadequate and unserviceable speculation houses, lacking in site orientation, durability, beauty, privacy and functionality. For each truly contemporary house there shoot from the defenseless ground a dozen boxes, held together by no more than Federal Loan Certificates (Plate 9). They are to serve today's land

9. REAL ESTATE DEVELOPMENT, NEW YORK STATE

settlers who, like birds, follow an instinct for survival in a better climate than that provided by the modern city: "The chimerical dream of individual liberty that obsesses those millions who want to walk once more with their feet in the green grass of nature"[3] has sent the disillusioned migrant in search of a personalized physical and social environment. These dreamers do not listen to statistics, offered by planners and theoreticians, that the individual detached house is as obsolete as the shaving mug and as disproportionate to their financial resources as the Hope Diamond. *Home ownership is an act of faith with man,* and, as all matters of emotion, is impervious to logic. It is a dangerous fallacy, cherished by most successful architects, that by ignoring its existence the small low-cost house will vanish from the earth. Its ugly imprint on the landscape is largely due to the lofty assertion that no architect is needed for its design, as if a doctor were to attend only to the births of future board chairmen while a midwife were good enough for truck drivers and stenographers.

According to a Public Housing Administration report, quickly outdated because there is a constant increase in the quoted figures,[4] a minimum of 7 million dwellings out of an existing 46 million in the United States are substandard and must be replaced in the immediate future. Our national income has risen so much that a 300% increase in the demand for $22,000 homes has been created which so far has been met by only a 30% increase in production. Without any attempt at reorientation of design standards, this combination of decay and need plays into the hands of the building promoter who has no inhibitions about ruining the American landscape for the sake of rapid investment returns. He knows what to make of the unhappy coincidence of architectural neglect and romantic ignorance by dangling, for instance, before the eyes of the new land settler a pasteboard replica of the Abraham Hasbrook House, built in 1712 (Plate 10) as if this were what today's family needs. For its location and times this Huguenot home was a marvel of functionality and good design. Its exceptional

[3] Le Corbusier, *When the Cathedrals Were White.* (Reynal and Hitchcock, 1947).
[4] National Municipal Revue, October 1955.

10. LEVITTOWN SPECULATION HOUSE

10. ABRAHAM HASBROOK HOUSE, NEW PALTZ, N. Y.

length of over sixty feet was due to an outsized kitchen where weekly cockfights at high bets scandalized the neighboring Puritans and entertained the French Patentees. The small window openings, flush with the roof plate to save on masonry, the steep roof pitch, the two feet stone walls were all adaptations of the medieval European farmhouse to a new environment of heavy precipitation and snowfall, poor heating provisions and unsafe territory open to Indian attack. It would be only logical if the speculator, disguised as benefactor, would offer together with television antenna, useless attic, and imitation wood shingles, a unionized detachment of attacking Seminoles to justify his fraud.

Architects of reputation have approached the small house problem via industrial prefabrication. Together with learned treatises on their inevitability and beauty, factory-built houses of plywood panels, plastic, sprayed rubber balloons, geodesic triangles and processed bamboo sprouts have been offered as the "home of tomorrow" (Plate 11). The fact still remains that the anonymous homeseeker will settle for a shoddy illusion of a designed home rather than for "a demonstrable increase in performance increments." Industrially produced containers, lined up on a bulldozed furrow, are too reminiscent of the city tenement he has fled, no matter how famous the name of the inventor or how original the construction material. And the savings are small, because even an ignorant prospective buyer gradually comprehends that the major expense of a house lies not with its walls and roof but with the lot, foundation and mechanical equipment.

It is not the repetition of type to which the home buyer objects in prefabricated houses. If he did, all our developments would stand empty. He has an instinctual aversion to their gross ugliness that does not permit even a tenuous illusion of designed environment. The history of domestic building shows that diversity in similarity is workable and attractive, provided that high standards of construction and taste are maintained. The old quarters of Savannah, Charleston, Germantown and Salem furnish proof. Plate 12 shows an example of early 19th century houses in Cap Haitien. The success of the historical

11. DYMAXION HOUSE BY BUCKMINSTER FULLER, ERECTED IN NORTH CAROLINA, 1940

row house lies in an acknowledgment of physically uniform requirements, inherent in man's biological sameness, and of psychologically variable requirements, inherent in man's individuality. The practical premise of building technology and the automation of household functions is taken for granted today. No one advocates a new primitivism of construction and equipment, but it is a degrading paucity of professional ability in the architect if he champions industrial prefabrication, disguised as social philosophy, for the sole purpose of quick investment returns. To strip down life to the "rationalized" provisions of a standard box reduces the human being to the sole aspect of biological uniformity. The individual is denied his superiority and it is this denial that has produced a curious reversal of the role of architecture. Where before a man selected or built a house to fit his unique needs; now he is urged by the most famous architects of the century to contort his whole existence to fit the provisions of the mass-produced technological shelter.

It has been argued that the study of historical prototypes—academic or indigenous—will not help the situation but might contaminate pure modern design with imitation. Imitation, it is true, transforms the past into a junk yard where parts of discontinued models can be picked up for re-use. It is not imitation that justifies an intense study of the past. It is inspiration that is urgently needed. Inspiration is an indispensable element of all growth, an intuitive response to related problems that are successfully solved. It derives from the eminent prototype an understanding of that which is timeless as against that which is timebound. Imitation concerns itself only with external form, inspiration with the total concept. Every creative effort is a metamorphosis of the spirit that must be fed on the admired precedent. It betrays the immaturity of an arrogant age to hail modern architecture as being "not a branch of an old tree but a new growth coming directly from the roots."

A fruitful appreciation of concept and quality in historical architecture is made easier for the layman in anonymous rather than in pre-designed buildings. Even the simplest settler house in its own setting

12.  STREET IN CAP HAITIEN, HAITI

furnishes concrete answers to human aspirations that are common to mankind. It is *sinnfaellig* (evident to the senses) representing a microcosmos of the totality of life. The best modern architecture, on the other hand, has the measure of its perfection outside the immediate reality of the building itself. The development and convictions of the architect who built it should be known to understand his design and the inevitable imperfections in realization. Only by knowing the prototypes from which he evolved and the ultimate goal· for which he is set, can the extent of his achievement be evaluated. These are factors open only to the trained mind while an indigenous and intuitive work of architecture is, as Goethe said of folk art, "like a word of God, spoken this instant."

In spite of all-out attempts to align architecture with the contemporary ideal of "quick turnover and ready replacement" we have to face the fact that house designing, like child bearing, is a creative activity that cannot be accelerated without destructive results. The consequences of both continue to reach into the future, whether what was conceived is permanently adequate and beautiful or permanently defective and ugly. Every human being and every building exert environmental influences beyond the control and lifetime of their creator. It is this unbreakable tie with the future that makes the historical vista imperative. Because "only by taking on infinitesimally small units for observation and attaining to the art of integrating them with the whole can we arrive at the laws of history."[5] In anonymous architecture, these units of observation concern themselves with four aspects which emphasize the contrast to pre-designed or technological building:

One: The unsupplemented use of native building materials and local construction skills.
Two: Planning and massing as the result of specific unduplicable functional requirements and site conditions, regardless of symmetry or generally accepted taste canons.

[5] Tolstoy, *War and Peace*.

44

Three: Absence of any ornamentation that is not part of the structure.
Four: Identity of enclosing form and enclosed space.

These are characteristics which can also be found in some modern designed buildings, but it is the purity of their expression that indicates the native builder. The clearest distinction between European village architecture and that of the American settlements is exemplified by these four points. In the Old World the application of decorative motifs, religious or secular, stressed submission to the church by invoking through signs and symbols divine protection, and the anonymous design repeated, almost automatically, traditional patterns of stylized forms (Plate 13). There also develops in post-medieval village and

13. WALL DECORATIONS IN MITTENWALD, GERMANY

town houses a "classical" tendency, adhering to a strictly axial plan, regardless of interior space distribution (Plate 14). It was a conscious emulation of the taste of the ruling class. The anonymous builders of the New World had no state religion and no Palladio to go by. They spun the sheltering skin around the inner space like a cocoon. The plan can be read from the walls as if they were transparent (Plate 15).

14.
16TH CENTURY INN,
SWITZERLAND

15.  CHURCH AT TRAMPAS, NEW MEXICO

Any attempt to present the existing wealth of vernacular buildings on this continent can be no more than an introduction, a mere sampling. Each example shown in this book is characteristic but it is not necessarily the best in existence. An unknown number of houses have never been recorded and are vanishing fast under the victorious bulldozer. They defy the cataloguing zeal of the historian. All classifications applied to anonymous architecture must remain arbitrary and unsatisfactory. It is the very nature of an intuitive work that it expresses all characteristics of its kind with faultless coherence. It was merely for the sake of concise presentation that the material was organized into three main groups, based on the principal criteria of *expression of site and climate, expression of form and function, expression of materials and skills.* These groups form the three sections of this book. They try to answer at least in part the where, why, and how of anonymous architecture.

# SITE AND CLIMATE *part two*

# SITE AND CLIMATE

When we speak of a "desirable" building site, we usually mean *location*, related to supply centers, communication, and real estate values. *Site* is actually something else. It is part of the physiognomy of the earth, a combination of features that make a piece of land as distinctive as a human face. The reaction produced in the land-taker by these indigenous characteristics sharply separates the settler from the speculator. The speculator lines up bulldozers and cement mixers and then poses the challenge: "What can I do to the land?" The settler asked: "What can the land do for me?" Where we use technology to subdue nature, the settler reached the same goal by observation and coordination. Like a hunter he stalked the site. Gradually he came to know all its assets and shortcomings, and he coordinated them according to the image of the final settlement.

The land-taker of the New World never shared the intensely spiritual concept of Oriental people toward the site. Chinese "Wu Wei," the reverential passivity that will not disturb nature, was at all times alien to him; and he would have justly doubted modern site mysticism that tries to revive: "the ancient's thought that the vital assets (of the site) were spirits. By listening intently you can hear them miraculously breathe in their slumber. You may subtly awaken them to startling values of design."[6] If the settler called in a divinator it was to locate water not to determine beneficial transits. His relationship to the land was that of a young organism to the parent body, challenging but dependent. He never hesitated to assert himself by carefully adjusting not only house to site but site to house as well. Had he known it, the settler would have agreed with Wright's proud and humble definition that "man takes a positive hand in creation whenever he puts a building upon the earth beneath the sun. If he has birthright at all, it must consist in this: that he too is no less a feature of the landscape than the rocks, trees, bears and bees of that nature to which he owes his being."[7]

Site, however, is meaningless without the complementary reality of *climate*. Site was selected and adjusted; climate had to be conquered. There is as much difference between climate and weather as there is between site and location. Weather is the local expression of climate. It is as variable and unpredictable as the moods of the heart and it changes just as quickly. The settler accepts this irresoluteness stoically. The modern city dweller's desire to be roasted indoors when it is cold outside, and to shiver artificially when the season is hot is alien to the settler, but the permanent conditions of climate he challenged to a contest with the same mixture of cunning, boldness and humility with which he adjusted settlement to site. Climate varies only slightly over the centuries. The changes it effects in large land masses are so imperceptible that the responses of the anonymous builders remained the same for many generations. It is in these responses that two outstanding characteristics of settler architecture become most evident: *diversity of solutions* and *transformation of handicaps into assets*.

Observation registers every wind direction, the cycle of light and shadow, the rise and fall of hot and cold air, but it is *brauch* that hands down the means of utilizing the absorbent and reflecting properties

[6] R. Neutra, *Mysteries and Realities of the Site*. (Morgan and Morgan, 1951).
[7] Frank Lloyd Wright, *An American Architecture*. Edited by Edgar Kaufmann (Horizon Press, 1955).

of materials, their resistance to rain and snow, and their composition for maximum climatic comfort. The difference between the climatic wisdom of an anonymous builder and the acquired learning of a mechanical engineer is merely a matter of implementation. The problems at hand, the natural laws observed, and the desired end result are essentially the same. The technical solutions of air conditioning and heating differ little throughout the world. It is therefore a startling discovery to find no two identical solutions of climate control among anonymous builders. From the woven huts of the Mexicans to the shingled barns of the North, the practical imagination of the settler is unlimited.

The site, then, gives to a structure its roots in the ground; it acts as orientator, relating house to landscape and to other settlements. Climate is a collateral form-giver. It influences the rhythm of mass and perforation. We are hardly conscious of this fact, but the shape and placing of openings is the second most decisive characteristic of its architecture, the first being the actual spot on which it stands. The simplest and the most sophisticated designs exert their esthetic influence on the environment through the balance of wall enclosure and wall opening. Animals achieve outstanding wall construction, as the bee in the hive cells, and so do some of the most primitive pit-house dwellers of semi-nomadic societies. But the only wall openings known to them are for access and exit. Fenestration is an emphatically humanistic achievement. Windows, according to the Germanic word origin, are "the eyes of the wind"; they look in and look out. The anonymous builder, alternating between exposing and shutting away the interior of the house, establishes multiple contacts between the defined and controlled space within and the unbounded natural space without. The placing of openings in the solid mass is determined by interior function but it is qualified by site, climate, and an innate sense of proportion, which act as modifying influences on frequency, size and orientation. A house exterior can invite or reject simply by the indication of its windows (Plate 16), and they tell the story of the land from which the owner came. In Central and South America the tale of Spain is told mainly by windows and doors. On a hacienda with the lovely name

16. MANSION, AUBURN, N. Y., 1813

55

17. WINDOWS, "PLACE OF THE HUMMINGBIRD," HUITZILTEPEC, MEXICO, 17TH CENTURY

"Place of the Hummingbird," Huitziltepec, near Zaragoza, Mexico (Plate 17), the hooded Andalusian window (Plate 18) has been recreated, although in the narrow streets of a medieval town the function of this window was different. It had to substitute for a balcony or a bay window, and its high socle assured privacy and safety. In Mexico there was no need for either. Consequently, the socle vanished, but the protecting hood that kept the rain away from the opening was retained.

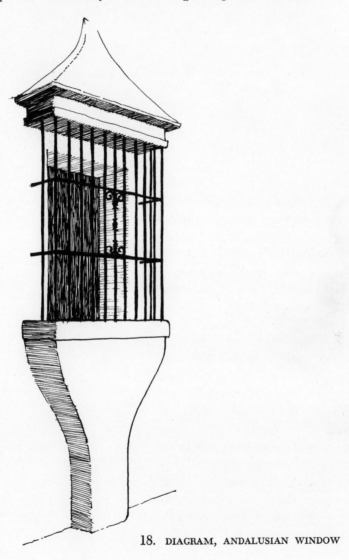

18.  DIAGRAM, ANDALUSIAN WINDOW

## 19

HACIENDA NEAR PUEBLA, MEXICO (19)

This plate and the following one are studies in harmony and contrast. The hacienda is camouflaged in its environment, as if its builders had carefully selected the rhythmic point in the relationship of plain to hill that would absorb the human settlement. The perfect accord of roof lines and hill lines is by no means accidental. The huge barn and storehouse in front is close to the road for easy access, while the wide, square yard beyond has the slight slope necesasry for drainage. The long, low structure to the right houses livestock, again taking advantage of the inclined ground. For the outside observer these are irrelevant considerations. What arrests the eye is a color scheme, ranging from the deep ochre of the buttressed brick barn to a delicate yellow, typical for adobe work, to the mottled grey of the heavy stone masonry, melting away into the hillside.

58

SITE AND CLIMATE: Landscape

## 20

VILLAGE PIAZZA, COSTILLO, NEW MEXICO (20)

The adobe buildings of this American bor-
der village and the encircling wall are raised
on the edge of a plateau to define clearly and
unequivocally the boundaries of human hab-
itation. There is no sharp contour, rather a
gentle, languid gesture that draws the human
line. The wide sun-baked village plaza accom-
modates herds and fiestas, but most of all it
gives a feeling of defined space, a generous
openness that fits the proportions of this spaci-
ous landscape. The angular forms of the light
yellow buildings seem moulded after the dis-
tant but dominant shape of the table mountain, which belongs to the Saor Amendo
Range. The settlers, Mexican in origin and
stolid of temperament, "render with natural
feeling" what is theirs. They neither feel a
need to transform their environment nor to
submit to it. They are in total accord with the
respective functions of man and nature.

SITE AND CLIMATE: Landscape

COURT OF AN OLD GRANGE NEAR LA MALABIE, QUEBEC, CANADA (21)

Even the simplest homesteads of French Canada echo in some feature nostalgia for a France lost. Everywhere in Quebec the architecture seems to be unreconciled to the new continent. French heritage and American landscape still seem to fight it out with each other. The Mexican granjero had taken up the rhythm of the intrinsic site as his natural support. The Canadian *propriètaire* still "forces nature" in the tradition of the *grand siècle*. He has cleared a window into space and framed it with French poplars that emphasize in their gaunt verticality the dividing line between the manoir and the open land. The weathered sandstone basin, flanked by two marble lions whose baroque forms seem strangely out of place in a simple farmyard, underlines the contrast with the land. This is a piece of France, a human landscape related to its natural site by emphasized nonconformity.

62

SITE AND CLIMATE: Landscape

FARM IN THE FOOT HILLS OF THE DIABLO RANGE,
CALIFORNIA (22)

This farmstead is protected by the folded hills as if a team of watchdogs were guarding its gate. The short well-grazed sward shines like smooth pelts, with the fence like a leash laid gently on their backs. The last dip beyond the hills and a thick clump of fruit trees shield the buildings from the road. The houses lie in the hollow as if they rested in the lap of creation. The inclusiveness of the site signifies both self-sufficiency and land control—the aspirations of all settlers fulfilled in a perfect setting.

It is more than topography that makes this site interesting. It gives historical evidence of two different systems of land tenure in the United States which separate the East from the West more distinctly than 200 years of history. The land in the East, particularly in New England, was granted by the English Crown to trading companies, and occasionally to worthy vassals, who in turn parcelled it out to groups of immigrants. The result was closely knit communities or closely related single farms with a tendency to uniformity in architecture. Hindered by the limited Open Field system, the New England farmers quickly turned traders and artisans for additional support. The symbols of their prosperity and communal pride became rather the buildings than the land.

In the West most rural settlements, as we see them today, originated after 1850 in the Land Grant and the Homestead Law periods. A basic parcel of 640 acres was sold by the Public Domain for $1.25 to $2.00 an acre. Even at that price the government found few takers, but those who came had no difficulty acquiring "kingsize" ranches, land holdings that stretched over the horizon. The pride of the Western settler is in his land which he still loves to imagine as being practically without boundaries. It is this sense of space which explains why the settlement buildings are centrally located. They lack, however, that special sense of permanence characteristic of the East. Tomorrow the rancher may acquire more land and then he will move his headquarters to a new central point of control.

64

SITE AND CLIMATE: The Inclusive Site

CHURCH AT WOUNDED KNEE, SOUTH DAKOTA (23)

The California farm shown in Plate 22 demonstrates a building site ideal for the Western rancher. This church tells of the ideals of the missionary. There exist thousands of similar Gothic Revival wood buildings all over the continent. Except for its smallness, this chapel has no indigenous characteristics. It is a routine carpenter's job. What gives it distinction is the selectiveness of its site. It arrests the eye with the authority of a cathedral. There is far and wide no other rise in the dead-flat wheatland. Only this bare knoll, lovingly observed and sought out by the congregation, could give prominence to their small edifice. It is a superb spot from which to signal The Cross and The Faith to the scattered homesteads, dotting the Great Plains like stars in a gigantic sky. To the west lies a Sioux Reservation almost sixty miles away, and the gilded cross on the needle-sharp steeple can be seen that far in the unhazed air. The achievement of the Neolithic settlers in separating physical from spiritual environment has here its simple and immensely effective American echo.

SITE AND CLIMATE: The Exclusive Site

In 1802 Napoleon massed 86 ships and 22,000 soldiers against the rebellious colony of Saint Dominique. In 1804 he abandoned the campaign and left General Henry Christophe to become the second Emperor of the Negro State, Haiti, born from the massacre of the French by the fabulous liberator Toussaint. Henry Christophe was 40 years old then and haunted by the sentence with which he started each day: "So much to do and so little time!" In 1802 he began La Citadelle, raised like an iron fist, on a summit 3,000 feet above sea level, with a ship's prow, jutting 130 feet over the crest of the slope toward the Plaine du Nord and the hated realm of the white man. For 18 years more than 5,000 men shaped this enormous symbol of Henry Christophe's challenge from the raw rock on which it stands. No building materials were imported; no tools but those of the local building trade were available. Like an amphora on the potter's wheel, the walls were raised with the bare hands of the builders above the narrow summit.

Neither Henry nor his mulatto engineer Henri Besse had ever seen a European fortress. "The Blacksmith's Pouch," as the people called the dark mass, was built by sheer intuition and a staggeringly costly process of trial and error. The walls rise 80 to 130 feet above the foundations and are 20 to 30 feet thick. Their building material is roughly dressed fieldstone, interlaced with brick, an *opus mixtum* as solid as that of the walls of Rome. To this day not an arch has sagged nor a wall tumbled. The adjustment to the site is perfect.

24. DIAGRAM, AERIAL VIEW OF FORTRESS LA FERIÈRE

The irregular mass is reenforced by the inward batter of the foundation and semicircular towers, which act as braces.

There were revolts when the emperor decimated a working team for laziness, and when the powder magazine of the nearly finished fortress was hit by lightning which demolished a whole wing. But Henry Christophe, who could not write or read, was stronger than the combined force of his subjects. The English envoy to the strange court of Sans Souci, with its courtiers and court ritual patterned after the *Ancien Régime* of Versailles, relates how on moonlit nights the emperor would ride on his white stallion to the top of the mountain, and there, alone, would dress stone and lay brick till dawn. In 1820, felled by a stroke and no longer in control of his exhausted and resentful subjects, Henry Christophe killed himself. *La Ferière* remained as unfinished as the battle for racial equality, but even as a ruin it is the most impressive indigenous building of the Western Hemisphere.

SITE AND CLIMATE: The Defensive Site

If La Ferière is all challenge, this monastic settlement, founded in 1732, is all withdrawal —withdrawal from hostile co-settlers, withdrawal from the Indians, and withdrawal from the temptations of the material world. The prophet who came to the Pennsylvania wilderness was a German pietist named Conrad Beissel. He had fled from community life to become a hermit, but was persuaded by those who wanted to be led to build a monastic retreat. The "Anabaptists of the Seventh Day" arranged their buildings on a slight ground swell, separated from the road by a wide, cleared meadow. Like horses in a corral under attack, the entrance façades of the main buildings face around a closed court, while expandable outbuildings are strung out along the Cocalico River.

Beissel and most of his followers came from the Palatinate and Alsace, and it was from there that they took their building pattern. The ancient hospital of Strasbourg has a high-pitched roof with dormers, cut irregularly into the slope where interior light was needed (Plate 27). The same roof is recreated in eastern Pennsylvania, but, with the natural intuition of the settler it has been locally adapted rather than mechanically repeated. The heavier precipitation of the Western Hemisphere called for an overhang of the shingled roof that would protect the planked wall and the window openings below, and each chimney stack is protected against the snow by its own wood shingle roof. The open gallery has been omitted and each of the

70

SITE AND CLIMATE: The Defensive Site

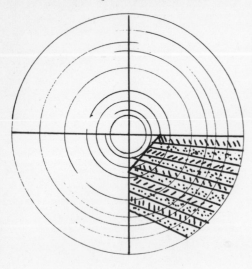

Ephrata buildings has an entrance porch. The roof shingles are made of cypress which is almost indestructible. (New York's oldest sewer pipes were hollowed cypress logs that lasted for almost 200 years.)

The clapboard on the "Saal," or assembly hall, to the left shows its later origin. It is wide, or "flat sawn," which means that the log is sliced through the way a modern power saw cuts tree trunks. The "Sister's House" to the right, one of the oldest buildings of the settlement, has "quarter-sawn" boards (Plate 28), cut against the grain from quartered trunks. The boards are narrow and short but impervious to warping. Each board is slightly thickened at the exposed edge. With wood plentiful and labor free, the early Ephrata settlers did not mind the waste inherent in this method or the laborious process of the tapered cut.

27. DIAGRAM, OLD HOSPITAL, STRASBOURG, FRANCE

72

SITE AND CLIMATE: The Defensive Site

29. DORMER ROOF, EPHRATA

In the *Atharva Veda* the Hindu deity is addressed thus: "I have crowned you with a shooting sugar cane so that thou shalt not be averse to me"; and a Roman poet speaks of "sweetness from the earth." In the middle of the last century, this sweetness was the wealth of the West Indies. In 1840 St. Croix exported 9,600 tons of sugar, 1,109,000 gallons of rum and 2,100 gallons of molasses. Eight years later the emancipation of the slaves destroyed the plantations where this wealth grew, and 25 years later the first mechanical sugar beet refinery killed what was left. The mills of that prosperous era still stand, impressive examples of settler skill in devising a type of building as new and experimental as the automobile factory was in 1900.

The ground in this region is unreliable because earthquakes are a continuous threat everywhere in the Caribbean. Thus the walls are tapered inward, the way the Egyptians used to taper their pylons. Another safety device is an interior earth core (Plate 30) that had a twofold purpose. It carried the grinding mechanism of two meshing stone rollers, set in motion by a windmill, and it filled the lower part of the opening. The cylindrical stone wall is put over it like the chimney of a lamp. The tall sugar cane was fed through the vertical opening, excessively high for its purpose, but magnificently effective as articulation of the grey monumental mass. The tower stands on a hill, exposed to the wind from all sides, a landmark for the seafarer, and, in times past, a gathering place for the workers in the cane fields.

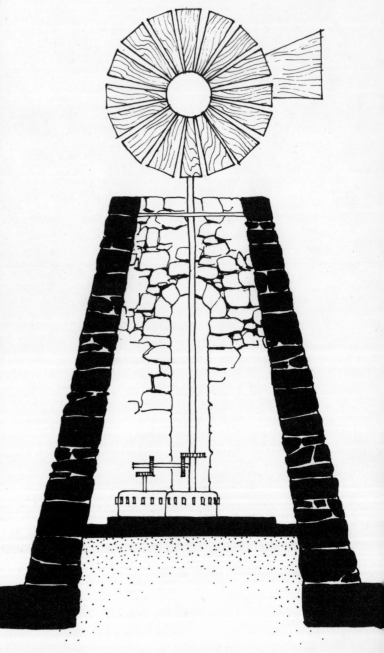

30. DIAGRAM, SECTION THROUGH SUGAR CANE MILL, SHOWING CRUSHING MECHANISM

**74**

SITE AND CLIMATE: The Working Site

The history of mills is a peculiar chapter in settler building because the grinding of grain is man's oldest mechanical invention, older even than the potter's wheel. The harnessing of natural power for the service of man was the first step toward technology. Water-driven mills far antedate windmills. The famous story of how the invading Goths destroyed Rome's main aqueduct in order to stop the grain mills and starve the city is well known. It was the Romans who brought water mills to France and England. Windmills originated where there was no water—on the dry, shamal-blown plateau of Syria. The Crusaders learned the windmiller's trade on their way to Jerusalem in the land around Aleppo and are said to have built their own experimental mills first in Antioch which they held through the 13th century. In the long process of history, the locally conditioned reasons for the invention of mechanically operated grindstones got mixed up. It was the water-rich Dutch who became the builders of windmills while the gale-swept English stuck to water mills.

This grist mill built in the first years of the 18th century combines in true immigrant style the *brauch* of two nations. The Philipse Estate was purely Dutch because the first "Lord of the Manor" had been Stuyvesant's chief carpenter. Yet the new location was too well-suited for an undershot water wheel to stick to native mill practice. The mill was oriented toward a small stream, narrowed down to a canal, which is treated with the care befitting a *waterway*. The stonework along the edge of the lawn and along the curve of the inlet that leads the water to the mill-shed is set with a fine craftsmanship. Trees, well spaced, accentuate the edge of the river. This part of the grounds was rarely seen. The main house faces the other way and no path leads along the water. It is the entity of working process and site planning which gives to the mill its harmonious setting.

**76**

SITE AND CLIMATE: The Working Site

In the mid 1850's James Renwick, the architect of St. Patrick's Cathedral, designed New York's first kitchenette apartments which then were called "Garçonnières" after the New Orleans pattern. The cast iron railing and the ornamental arches were imported from the German Ruhr foundries, and the full-length French doors were a sensation in the big city. In our own age which exploits the building site to the last fraction of an inch for rental profit, this Victorian building evokes nostalgia. One is reminded of the fact that there was a time in architecture when landlord and designer combined their efforts to attract tenants by superior planning rather than "12 cubic foot refrigerators, colored bathroom tiling, television antenna and air conditioning outlet."

In winter the continuous balcony was an insulation against snow and cold. In summer, facing north, it was a cool outdoor room, looking down on a long garden strip of trees, flowering shrubs and lawn. There was no interior stairwell and rooms went the entire depth of the building, facing south in the rear with a full admission of sunlight, until the apartment skyscrapers blocked it out. There was more to this planning than merely the pleasure and comfort of the tenants. A city site so treated refreshed the passerby. It kept him in touch with the life of plants and birds. It made a whole city block as distinctly individual as a manor house or a farm. The cycle of the seasons is unrolled before the rootless town dweller.

78

SITE AND CLIMATE: The City Site

As the second largest coal producer in the United States, West Virginia has some of the worst slum settlements in the nation. In some of the earliest mining towns, which go back to the Civil War and the time when this part of Virginia seceded to join the Union, there exists a peculiar type of coal-town architecture. It blends the tradition of the single dwelling with the need for multiple occupancy. The man who built this tenement could have glued it precariously and impermanently against the mountainside as did his neighbors. Instead he accepted the disadvantage of the steep lot and made it into something unique and beautiful. He had no bulldozers to level the ground into uniformity. He had to build up his foundations with careful consideration of the stability inherent in his materials. The result is a base that rises in four distinct accents. The street wall with its handsome joints of irregular boulders is surmounted by the lively color line of trimmed shrubbery. Above it rises the pleasantly proportioned concrete stair wall, terminated by the field-stone socle of the house itself.

Such an explicitly varied use of materials and methods must have been chosen by a man with an architectural sense for structural as well as esthetic precision. The total impression is one of quality, and the viewer is led to expect a more monumental climax, but even the modest frame dwelling atop all this careful piling shows thought and planning. The Spanish gallery around all four sides of the house has been used to avoid an interior stairwell.

The end effect, however, offers more than mere economy. The long loggia permits a wide vista of the mountains beyond the mines. A child, growing up in this simple dwelling, would feel happy by the inclusion of hills, rivers, wood and sky in his daily experience.

80

SITE AND CLIMATE: The City Site

*Of the five climatic zones of the earth's surface, only two have an actual influence upon settler architecture in this hemisphere. The Temperate or Variable Zone extends from the Polar Circle southward to the Tropic of Cancer that passes south of Miami and divides Mexico. The other is the Torrid or Equatorial Zone, stretching south to the equator. Every settler will tell you that these divisions are mere theory and without practical meaning. There is nothing temperate about Canadian snow and mid-western heat; and the torrents of rain which are native to the Mexican plateau do not fit the torrid zone. The settler has his own climatology that deals with the four climatic conditions he has to combat: cold, snow, rain and heat. For him this is weather and all there is to climate. His adjustments are geared to these phenomena.*

The Achaean settlers of Greece brought from
the north to the Mediterranean the Megaron.
It was a totally new type of dwelling which
differed greatly from the flat-roofed, mud-
brick structures of the Mesopotamian and
Egyptian civilization. This one or two room
house was square because it was built of
timber. A wide porch must have been the most
pleasant part of the house because all through
the songs of Homer it is offered to the honored
guest as sleeping quarters. The pitched roof
of sloping rafters was supported by columns
made of sturdy tree trunks. The triangular
pediment, formed by architrave beam and
sloping rafters, was left open, divided only by
the kingpost which carried the ridge pole on
each end. From the earliest model at Pera-
chora to the splendid hall of the Mycenaean
Kings, the Megaron house remained un-
changed.

This cabin, high in the Rockies, is a pure
image of the ancient Greek prototype: the
same spacing of porch supports, the same
left-sided placing of the entrance, the same
architrave beam and kingpost, dividing the
open pediment triangle. The only important
variation from ancient *brauch*, showing adjustment to the new surroundings, is the "pine
moss" roof which is of Scandinavian origin.
The settlers of America went after each tree
with a vengeance which prompted Isaac Weld
from Dublin to write home in 1796: "These
people have an unconquerable aversion to
trees. . . ." But for the sake of climatic advantage they left a few tall pines standing as close
as possible to the house. When the needles
shed, they accumulated between the pine
rafters, gradually forming a sod base from
which grew a dense covering of grass. "Pine
to Pine" was what the old mountain builders
called this process, saying that pine needles
would not decay pine logs or boards, and
knowing that the sod roof would be an ideal
insulation against snow in winter and heat in
summer.

**84**

SITE AND CLIMATE: Cold

OLD POWDER STORAGE HOUSE, OURAY, COLORADO
(36)

Next to cold which threatens the settler of
the temperate zone so intemperately, snow is
his greatest enemy. The two problems are
weight and seepage. Both are met with intuitive skill in this powder magazine. It dates
most probably from the second half of the
19th century, judging by its iron door and the
wrought iron hinges, set without door framing
into the stone wall itself. Actually a shell of
fieldstone and mortar it encloses its precious
contents with the perfection of an egg.

It was said earlier that "economy of resources and upkeep" is one of the three human
achievements in the conquest of chaotic nature. This structure is a good example of this
principle. The barrel vault, a semi-circle with
irregular corner voussoirs anchoring it to the
wall, is finished to complete smoothness because it is here that the greatest snow-load has
to be expected. The walls whose function is
strength and not evenness have been left to
their natural texture of grey granite chunks,
set with white lime mortar. Snow could en-
tomb this structure but it could never en-
danger the interior.

86

SITE AND CLIMATE: Snow

This closed-down cotton mill from the middle of the last century bears witness to the fact that the early factories and tenements were built by the same craftsman who, before, had built homesteads and barns. The gable especially conforms to the best Dutch brick tradition. There is an intricate herring-bone pattern at the points of greatest stress. A double molding of white stone runs along the lower roof line and ends visibly, in the manner of coping stones, where the brick gables need support. It is a building with a profile, like the profile of a distinctive and determined face. One can imagine the agreeable *en face* of the whole structure before the loading shed was thoughtlessly and brutally pushed against the fine elevation.

The climatic response of this early factory design is particularly interesting, because it combines a purely esthetic pleasure with weather protection and the use of interior space. The break between the lower and the upper gable-ends disperses the load of the snow. It is a device of great antiquity, known all over the north and east of Europe. The most celebrated examples of snow-break roofs are the Norwegian stave churches (Plate 37) which sometimes have three or four breaks to lighten the wintry load. In this Vermont structure a clearstory is set between the breaks to utilize every ray of daylight for the mill interior—a design feature unknown to the medieval Scandinavians. The combination of load-reducing and light-increasing design has created a building contour that has all the grace of a "baroque" elevation without being decorative.

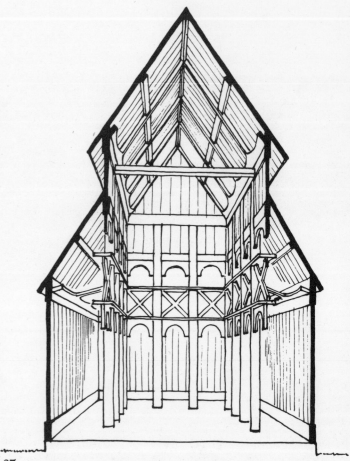

37. DIAGRAM, SECTION THROUGH A NORWEGIAN STAVE CHURCH

SITE AND CLIMATE: Snow

TWO BARNS ON THE RESERVATION OF FORT KLA-
MATH, OREGON (39)

The East of the United States developed salt-box houses to accommodate the kitchen under the same roof as the living quarters. The West has a special type of saltbox barn which is a purely climatic invention. The long slant of the roof faces "into the weather," meaning in the direction of the prevailing wind. The roof ends four or six feet above the ground. In winter, during the time of maximum snowfall, the space between lower roof edge and ground was filled with bales of hay or alfalfa to form a natural continuation of the snow blanket, covering the roof. The purpose is exactly opposite of that in Plate 38. The stout oak frame construction and the slant of the roof are calculated to accumulate a protective snow load rather than to disperse it.

The south walls of these two barns have another thermal device: they are painted bright red. When farmers started to paint their buildings in the early 19th century there was no "store-bought" paint. Skim milk was mixed with oxide of iron—rust, to wit, scraped from fences and nails—and with lime. The result was a sort of varnish that did not sink into the wood grain but covered it like a skin. When it peeled, it came off in large rubbery patches. The choice of red was by no means accidental. Because red absorbs sunlight, it was a "solar heat" device. The handicap of a region with severe winters has been turned into an advantage. The natural warmth of the animals inside the barn together with the natural provision of a protective snow layer on one side and heat-absorbing red on the other, are the calculated assets of husbandry in the north.

90

SITE AND CLIMATE: Snow

The native huts this man had seen on his voyages had taught him climatic lessons, but he did not build himself an imitation native house. He adapted aboriginal weather wisdom to his European heritage. The perforation of walls (shown later in this book in a variety of materials and techniques) has been achieved in jigsaw fretwork which is a curious mixture of Maori wood art and Victorian gingerbread. Its main function is not decorative but useful, for it shields the continuous balcony from public view and allows the cooling night winds to blow through. On the right side a loggia juts out, not over the hot and dusty road but over a jungle of palms and vines which admit a purer, fresher air. The house extends on all sides over a solid masonry core which, though almost dark, assures at all times a cool retreat. The tin roof, standard in all tropical countries, is painted white to reflect the heat.

This house, compared with the three following plates, furnishes an interesting contrast in the philosophy of life. Natives build lightly. The accent in all aboriginal houses is on flexibility, an elastic adjustment to environmental conditions, which allows for a quick retreat, unencumbered by walls or doors, if nature turns openly hostile. European immigrants, in contrast, cannot let go of the ancient settler concept of permanence. They emphasize wall and roof. The structure is clearly outlined against the natural environment. Durability is a matter of pride and investment. The native hut is a loose cloak for man; the European settler house is a solid armor.

SITE AND CLIMATE: Heat

The lean-to, it has been claimed, was the one original contribution to architecture made by the dour New England Puritans. This bamboo house has a typical lean-to, housing not the kitchen but the burro whose hoofs are kept dry by the self-draining slant of the floor. In sub-tropical regions heat and rain usually go together. Here each of the two weather excesses is handsomely and ingeniously taken into consideration. The walls are of split bamboo poles, neatly joined at the corners with palm trunks forming the interior corner posts. These posts are sharply pointed before being rammed into the ground. If a leak develops in the thatched roof, the posts are hammered a few inches deeper into the earth to close the gap.

The roof might look like an untidy haystack at first sight, but it actually is a carefully woven and shaped rain-shed. The steep pitch with a single ridge point distributes the water to all four sides of the curbed roof, but the most efficient drainage devices are flashings of long rice straw, hanging along the four ridges. They protrude some three feet over the porous house wall, conducting the water away from the main structure which remains an airy, dry, well-ventilated enclosure, no matter how severe the downpours.

94

SITE AND CLIMATE: Heat

There are two different kinds of heat in subtropical regions, one is permanent and the other cyclic. In the high mountain ranges of Haiti the days are blazing hot during the dry season, but the nights are cold. The *caille* in the mountains takes this cyclic condition into account. The walls are rubble and mud mortar, whitewashed with gypsum plaster to repell the heat. A door, as tall as the full height of the wall, admits the daytime warmth which rises into the steep gable of the roof. There it hovers like a warm blanket, lining the thick thatch, ready to cover the sleepers during the cold night.

The permanent heat lingers in the deep valleys, regardless of time of day or season, and it is reduced only by the breeze that sometimes sweeps down from the hills. In spite of Toussaint's "Haitian Vespers," which killed off the European oppressors, two distinctly French building elements were retained by the Negroes; one is the dormer and the other the French door. Both, although they originated in the European north for different reasons, are here used as climatic devices. The floor to ceiling opening admits light by day and air by night, but it is the central dormer that is most admirably adapted as ventilator. Supported by the posts of the porch, it overhangs the house wall and traps each breeze that might come its way, expelling the rising heat admitted through the French door (Plate 43).

The high conductivity of the corrugated tin roof allows for quick cooling off as soon as the sun has set, and it is completely termite proof. The walls are woven screens, joined seam to seam where privacy is wanted, and left half open directly under the dormer to increase the upward draft of air. We speak so much of functionality today that the word no longer has any meaning; here functionality is a total concept. There is no element in this simple settler house that does not serve the function of human comfort.

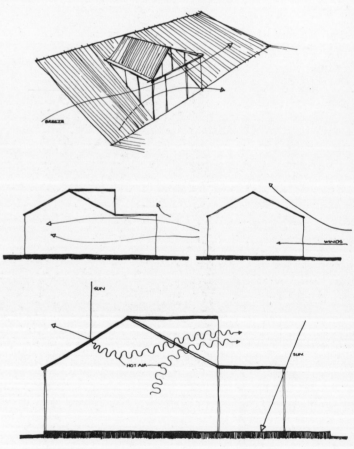

43. DIAGRAMMATIC PRESENTATION OF AIR CURRENTS IN PLATE 44

SITE AND CLIMATE: Heat

42

44

JACAL OR STRAW HOUSE, PUEBLA, MEXICO (45, 46)

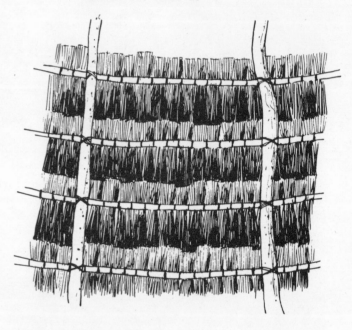

This flounced house stands on the road between Tequiquitla and Totlaxcala. These names are recorded here only because their exotic musicality seems to fit the character of this curious little dwelling. The exterior is as sophisticated as the flounced costume of a ballerina. Its interior is as primitive and primordial as the first pit-house: earth floor, a few steps below ground level, a small firepit on one end which is rarely used because life takes place out of doors if weather permits, and narrow benches, built up from rubble and mud binder, running along the walls as the only furnishings.

The interior framework (Plate 45) consists of "crucks," bent posts that are lashed together at the roof ridge, no different from the Anglo-Saxon cruck houses still standing in England today. A ridge pole extends the entire length of the house and forms the main support for the heavy tapestry of overlapping straw flounces. The sisal rope braiding is extremely precise and of a handsome evenness. In the interior a casual daubing with liquid mud here and there prevents the straw ends from turning up or being blown apart by the wind.

Every "half lifetime," so the owner said, the house gets too old for comfort. Then it is burned down among great festivities after a new one has been constructed exactly like the old one on the opposite side of the yard. The Japanese do the same with their most ancient and revered Shinto shrines. It may be that the Mexican native feels compelled—as does the Japanese—to retain through the endlessly re-created house an unbroken contact with his ancestors.

98

SITE AND CLIMATE: Rain

46

STREET IN PICHUCALCO, CHIAPAS, MEXICO (47, 48)
and OVERHANG, MAIN STREET OF HUATCHINANGO,
VERA CRUZ, MEXICO (49)

The Medido, or surveyor, was as important
in the days of the Spanish conquest as was the
Conquistador and the Padre. It was he who
determined the location of new settlements
according to beneficial wind directions which
had to be east-west on the coast and north-
south inland. Cortez hoped to build the communities of his New World according to the
"ideal town plans" of the Italian Renaissance
architects. By 1573 he was able to issue the
first urban planning law in the Americas. It
was based on Alberti's concept, formulated
one hundred years earlier, that "the house is
a civic function."

Each house owner was free to express his
individuality unchecked in the interior plan,
but the exterior had to be part of the "Casa-
Muro"—the continuous wall of houses standing like one rampart against the incessant
Indian uprisings. The continuous roof overhangs of the Casa-Muro run parallel rather
than at an angle to the prevailing wind and
protect the pedestrian during the rainy season.
In addition, each house owner was responsible for that part of the public domain on
which he bordered. Façades had to be of
stone, roofs had to be tiled and not thatched
to prevent conflagrations, and a stone curb,
three feet above the sewage channel, must
join with that of the neighbor. Town plazas
had to be twice as long as they were wide,
and streets had to have a minimum width of

47. DIAGRAMMATIC PRESENTATION OF ROOF
OVERHANG AND OF BUILDING ARRANGEMENT
IN PLATE 48

100

SITE AND CLIMATE: Rain

fifteen feet. The results of this master plan are towns that even today have a dynamic symmetry that is pleasing and serviceable.

Roof overhangs vary from town to town and even in adjoining quarters of the same town. In Pichucalco, the roof rafters (Plate 47) are carried down from the ridge of the house to meet evenly spaced columns of handsome proportions that are not the same in design but are similar. In Huatchinango, some overhangs (Plate 49) extend eight feet over the house wall without any exterior support. A white-washed shelf rests on the heavy ceiling beams of the interior, overshot by the roof rafters. Their golden brown staining contrasts agreeably with the red underside of the roof tiles. Like an umbrella, this undulated tile roof protects the sidewalk, depositing the flood of rainwater in the unpaved center of the street.

102

SITE AND CLIMATE: Rain

49

# FORM AND FUNCTION   *part three*

# FORM AND FUNCTION

Among anonymous builders there were as many bunglers who studded the land with eyesores as there are among today's architects. It might be assumed that their worst blunders, being unserviceable and shoddy, vanished fast. Some examples, however, survive and offer the inescapable conclusion that an anonymous building can be judged as good first of all by its *coherence*, by "a union of parts." It might seem academic to quote Vitruvius in this connection, but, despite its hoary age, his definition remains by far the finest one:

> "Proportion is the commensuration of the various constituent parts with the whole. For no building can possess the attributes of composition . . . unless there exists that perfect conformation of parts which may be observed in a well-formed human body."

Plate 50 shows a typical failure. This vernacular structure lacks coherence of parts and proportions. It is a careless accumulation of primitive shelter forms. Plate 54, on the other hand, offers an example of exceptionally fine coherence, relying not on symmetry but on composition.

The issue of Form versus Function has become virulent today; a pitched battle is fought between the Functionalists and the Formalists.

The Functionalists try to prove that a building's merit depends exclusively on the efficiency of its structure and its serviceable space. With Emerson they believe that "the true and the good must ultimately become the beautiful." The Formalists quote Alberti as their champion who saw in architecture "art as the cloak of beauty thrown over the bareness of matter." "Significance," expressed esthetically, is claimed as superior to function or construction. In this bewildering argument it will do good to go back to pre-conscious building, to the time before the architect had eaten from the tree of verbalization and in his innocence did not yet know how to separate form from function. His esthetic sense was automatic. He created with the artlessness of a pure conscience that looks for nothing but fulfilled purpose. This purpose included physical and spiritual needs. The form mediated between the strength of materials and the interior space. The ultimate solution was based on perception, the experience of reality through the senses.

50. POSSUM RUN CABIN, ALABAMA

Pre-designed, technological architecture, in contrast, is at its finest when it is conceptual, expressing an idea that dominates scientifically tested materials and construction methods. The generating force in the academically trained architect is his intellect; in the anonymous builder it is his intuition. This distinction defines their respective spheres of achievement. It can be illustrated with the example of ancient pottery. The making of vessels is closely related to architecture. Its aim, too, is structural and spacial coordination in the third dimension. Both testify by their primordial origin to an innate forming impulse. A specimen from the Orient and one from Greece are used here to demonstrate two different wills to form (Plate 51).

Oriental vessels are at their finest and most original when they express pure concept, pure idea—ceremonial, esthetic or symbolic. Their function is the expression of a ritual that has originated in the mind of man. If this idea is strong enough, the vessel becomes its

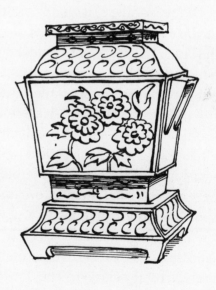

51. GREEK HYDRA AND CHINESE INCENSE BURNER

109

carrier. It can deny the structural law of the potter's wheel by being square or octagonal; it can break the unity of surface and void by applied and sculptured decorations, but it will not lose the significance of its idea. Form and function originate in the discriminating intellect.

Greek pottery originates from the opposite impulse. It is a fulfilled practical need, an empirical reality given form by the intuitive intelligence of the maker. It is based on pure function, expressed in the inextricable relatedness of the form that encloses and the hollow that contains, harmonized by the nature of the material and the process of creation on the wheel. Greek pots are first and foremost containers, whether they hold water or ashes. They are not created as esthetic or ritualistic symbols. No matter how great the delight of the maker in artistic perfection, he was in search of contained usefulness, fulfilling its purpose through a conscientious regard for raw material, working process and decorative surface treatment. A Greek Hydra and a Chinese Incense Burner can stand as symbols of the ideal relationship of form and function in architecture before and after *The Fall*.


Of the so-called "national landmarks" only a few have been included in this book because most of the widely acclaimed early buildings of the Americas were not spontaneously built. They expressed tradition, not *brauch*. The Canadian *manoir* is diluted Mansard, conspicuous proof of the owner's gentile background, as is the Georgian mansion from Cooperstown to Charleston. It was the poor man's dream of Campbell and Kent. The colonnaded plantation houses of the South either proclaim the classical revival of Soufflot and Vignon with a worshipful gesture to the Heroic Romanticism of the Napoleonic era, or they echo the Roman dream of Thomas Jefferson. They are not spontaneous adaptations to a new and challenging environment. Even the New England Saltbox (Plate 52) lacks the two qualifications: specific response to local environmental conditions and uniqueness of architectural solution. The Puritans who created this house type in the Western Hemisphere offer the peculiar historical paradox of being protesting conformers. They sacrificed all they possessed in order to save their individual consciences. From this enormous deed they derived a spirit of righteous kinship to God that found its expression in a dictatorial community spirit. The early New England house was a symbol of utter conformity with the non-conforming congregation. Just as women dress to impress men, so the Saltbox was built to impress the community with the undeviating righteousness of its inhabitant. The crystallization of a socio-economic and religious dogma eclipsed spontaneous architecture in America as it had done in Europe toward the close of the Middle Ages.

"Thought produces a generality of form" wrote Albertus Magnus in the 13th century, contemplating, perhaps with a suppressed yawn, the standard Gothic cathedral of the Rayonnant Period. Theocratic societies, since the days of Babylonia and Egypt, express themselves in prototype structures that receive their symbolic meaning from their standardized form of which the New England house is a late example. But the settlers who came to the Americas, not in groups, but as individuals, knew no other generator of architectural form than the need to shelter what they were and hoped to be. It is one of the fascinating aspects of architectural history on this continent that prototype structures, such as Saltbox and Meeting houses stand side by side with the spontaneous shelters, derived from an infinitely diversified concept of form and function.

52.  NEW ENGLAND SALTBOX, CONNECTICUT

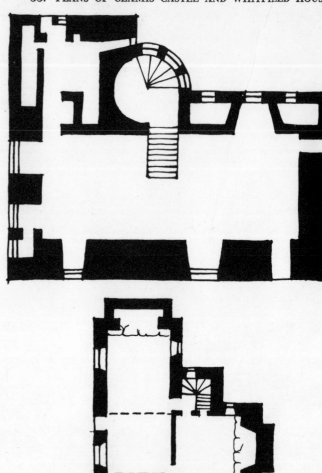

After the preceding statement on Puritan houses, the inclusion of this old stone house needs an explanation. It is analyzed here because it is the most remarkable domestic structure of the 17th century still standing in the United States. It had no exact prototype and has no successors. It is the pure undiluted response of a gifted individual to the challenges of a new environment with the resources of *brauch,* tradition and intuitive talent. All the successive stages of settler memory and settler innovation are successfully realized.

When the Connecticut Covenanters started this building in the same year in which they reached the Colonies, the innovations of Tudor architecture had been forgotten for 100 years, killed by the Italianizing Elizabethans and the dead hand of Inigo Jones. But the Reverend Whitfield carried in his remarkable head the memory of an architectural revolution that had been as far-reaching as the replacement of the Saxon Wood Hall with the Norman Keep of solid stone. This revolution was the emergence of a specifically domestic building concept that no longer took its forms and methods from reduced church prototypes.

We are told that the Reverend was British, but the inspiration for his stone house might have come from Glamis Castle in Scotland (Plate 53). This old stronghold had been radically remodelled in the late 15th century according to a plan that must have had an upsetting effect on the keep-and-dungeon aristocracy of the Highlands, similar to that of Wright's Coonley House on the style

poachers of Oak Park in 1900. In Glamis, the Tudor revolt against an outdated fortification pattern resulted in an ell-shaped layout that ignores enceinte and moat. It breaks through the heavy walls with many wide window openings and replaces the exterior access to the Solar with a solidly enclosed stair tower in the bend of the ell.

The Guilford house has the unheard of luxury of two staircases, an interior one, lead-

FORM AND FUNCTION: The Dwelling

ing to the well-designed second floor, and a stair tower in the bend of the ell. It permitted access to the upper story without crossing the first floor hall, an arrangement that was particularly useful for a building that had to serve as meeting house, barracks, tavern and living quarters. There are three luxurious fireplaces, and the large hall can be partitioned off by wood dividers, folding back against the ceiling on leather hinges (Plate 53). The three chimneys, unique for many years to come in the Colonies, are buttressed like the towers of English parish churches, such as Brampton.

Clapboard, that ubiquitous local material of all settlers, was not permanent enough for the Reverend. He uses it only on the north gable (Frontispiece). His house is built of dressed fieldstone, set with wide joints into a mortar of yellow clay and ground oyster shell (Plate 55) which is the Spanish *tapia*, a most unusual material for the north of this continent. Cartagena and San Marco in Florida were built with this binder which testifies to the far-flung contacts of the Covenanters and their exceptional open-mindedness to innovations.

With all its intelligent and comfortable affluence, the old stone house obviously did not satisfy the worldly Puritan who built it. In spite of the solemn covenant that bound the pioneers forever to the American soil, he found an excuse to return to England and never came back.

FORM AND FUNCTION: The Dwelling

55. CHIMNEY DETAIL, WHITFIELD HOUSE

This is the second of the four "national landmarks" included in this book for their special
significance. (The others: Ephrata, Pa.; Old
Stonehouse, Guilford; and Fort Edgecomb,
Maine.) The 17th century Dutch Manor of
Philipsburg once ruled 25,000 acres of Hudson Valley land from this fieldstone structure,
built in 1683. It is a house, not very different
from other Dutch and Flemish houses between
New York and Albany, although the departure
from the usual 45 degree roof pitch is a bold
innovation, based on the request of Lady
Philipse that her girl slaves live under the
same roof with her.

The moving message of this house comes
from the unselfconscious combination of old
and new. The old pioneer house and the adjoining Federal structure of exactly 100 years
later form an organic entity. The colonial
structure was not "modernized." Its entrance
remained through a trapdoor in the basement
that could be closed swiftly in the event of an
Indian attack. Its fireplaces remained the core
of the dwelling. In the new house the unob-
trusive adaptations of classical elements are
so tasteful that they are mere hints at a refinement reached by a noble family within two or
three generations. There is no attempt at symmetry. The interior room arrangement remains
the dominant factor in fenestration. Openings
are left and right of the central chimneys in
the old house; and, in the new one, on the
stair-landing and left and right from the two
end-wall fireplaces.

In Europe a peasant bares his head when
he passes the churchyard where his ancestors
lie. Here the passage of time, that great unifier
of contrasts, has been reverently acknowledged with a relatedness of form and function
that binds the new to the old. The non-urban
settlement is an accretion in time, like the
rings of a growing tree. Space had to be
widened and a growing complexity of human
relationships and living devices had to be
accommodated; but the old form continued to
serve in its limited capacity—useful to its
natural end like a healthy grandparent. Economy of resources and upkeep, one of the three
basic tenets of man as the builder of a selective environment, shrank back from a mechanical replacement of old matter with new
which did not improve on the desired purpose.

118

FORM AND FUNCTION: The Dwelling

TOWN HOUSE, CAP HAITIEN, HAITI (57)

In 1802 Henry Christophe, military leader under King Dessalines, knew that he could not prevent Napoleon's fleet from landing in Cap Haitien. Word had reached him that the French troops were accompanied by Napoleon's beautiful sister Pauline, her husband and her entourage, and that they planned to revive in the island the splendor and oppression of the *Ancien Régime*. When the ships landed, only 60 houses of the more than 800 remained standing. With his own hands Henry had set fire to a town that had no equal in the West Indies for the beauty of its buildings and public squares, its theatre and churches. When the French finally withdrew, ravaged by guerrilla warfare from the hills and jungles and by yellow fever, Henry started to rebuild the town he loved so much.

Today Cap Haitien has the charm and dignity of a Provençal town. Although its inhabitants are poor, the town houses, some 140 years old, stand without decay. None of the Baroque decorations that had adorned the façades of the burnt mansions were recreated. The houses of "Le Cap" are beautiful in their proportions, expressed in French doors, flared hip roofs, and the graceful balconies, joined to the overhang of the roof by delicate iron braces. The plaster of Paris walls are gaily but not loudy colored—lemon yellow, dusty pink, and particularly a heavenly blue. While the sun stands in the zenith, the six-foot roof overhang throws a deep shadow over the balcony, and whatever business has to be transacted is done there. At night, the high, iron-clad doors are flung wide open. Then the lifeless town block becomes a continuous arcade with family life spilling over the sidewalks as if this were Nice or Marseilles. The wrought iron railings stand out as graceful filigree against the warm light of the interior, and chatting couples lean contentedly against the gently rounded corner of the elegant old house. This corner and its superb craftsmanship, unchipped and unweathered in more than a century, emphasizes more than anything else could the contrast between Port-au-Prince, the Haitian capital in the south, and Cap Haitien in the north.

Port-au-Prince was built in fierce defiance, not only of the hated French Colonials but also of the "Northern Kings" of Haiti. The

120

FORM AND FUNCTION: The Dwelling

57

architecture of Port-au-Prince is a curiously temporary affair—gaunt stilts (Plate 58), carrying balconies and loggias in order to utilize each slight breeze and the cool air of night. It is functional but impermanent, shoddy but at the same time full of individual innovation. No two of these stilt-houses are alike, and none of them expresses the desire for refinement and permanence that is the French heritage of the Northern Haitians where old men still salute each other with the words "Respect et Honeur." It was the only redeeming deed of the plantation owners, that against their will they established in the New World a nucleus of Mediterranean architecture that has survived, almost forlornly, in this remote and inaccessible port of Cap Haitien.

122

FORM AND FUNCTION: The Dwelling

ACONA PUEBLO, NEW MEXICO (59) and HOUSE
OF THE TERRITORIAL PERIOD, CALIFORNIA (60)

In spite of the store-bought screen doors and glazed windows, this pueblo shows its original concept. Pueblo people, living together in their multi-roomed strongholds, are organized according to kivas, the sacred room in which religious ceremonies are observed. A kiva and its presiding shaman have very much the same function as the Christian Parish. The dividing walls between units, seen in the picture, are actually parish boundaries, but they are more than that. They are buttresses, giving strength to the terraced construction, and they are staircases, assuring vertical circulation of air. They define the mass horizontally and vertically, and they descend without break into the wall, encircling the lowest part of the settlement. The material is adobe, built up in pre-cast blocks which each year are plastered over with a liquid adobe mortar and then whitewashed to reflect the sun. The achievement of the adobe builders is total unity in structure and appearance and total separation in social units. Not "form follows function" but form is the servant of function.

The California house from around 1846 is also constructed of adobe. Its structural system shows a very different ancestry than the Indian Pueblo, whose *vigas*—the heavy horizontal timbers, serving as supports for the adobe roof—do not terminate in an architrave beam. In the Pueblo the many-layered covering is poured to the edge of the woven scantlings that are the roof base. In the California settler house the ancient European Megaron tradition asserts itself, as it had in the lumberman's cabin (Plate 35). The origin of the Doric entablature can be read from this structure as if it were meant to serve as an historical demonstration. The Doric column and the capital, with the saucer-like semicircle of the echinus and the flat end of the abacus, are recognizable, together with a hint how the Ionic volute might have grown from the Doric prototype. Here is the architrave beam in its double function of supporting the roof and linking bay to bay in what Frank Lloyd Wright once called: "the horizontal line of domesticity." Here is the origin of the dentils, the protruding ends of rafters or joists and the pure white band of the frieze, unadorned as in the archaic days of the Greek style. Here, in short, is the First Cause of *style* in architecture as the esthetic refinement of structural necessity.

FORM AND FUNCTION: The Dwelling

Form is function, as every settler house proves, but in some examples the truth of this statement is more evident than in others. At an altitude of 8,000 feet, the climatic problem for the Otomi Indian is twofold. It gets bitterly cold at night and there is a deadly shortage of water. Once he had risen beyond the planted cactus house, still widely used by the poorest of these poorest of all Mexican natives (Plate 5), he had to adjust his house to the unique conditions of a high plateau, offering only stone, cactus and maguey, and lacking timber, water or arable soil. Maguey was made into pulque which is—not for better but for worse—the staple food of man and child in this region. Stone became the great challenge for the builder. Lime for mortar is scarce and so are large boulders, suitable for spans. Building has to be done with the economy dictated by scarcities.

The walls are made of the stone surrounding the settlement, but its sizes vary with the structural function they have to serve. Door posts and lintels in a red sandstone brought from far away are surprisingly well shaped. They are the only concession to decorative craftsmanship and therefore doubly effective in their appearance. The largest native blocks available are used as quoins, set with alternate extension into both walls to assure a stronger grip. They also form those parts of the wall that have to carry the maximum stress of the stone roof. Lime is exceedingly scarce, so mortar has been restricted to these crucial areas of load. Below, where stability is assured by perpendicular pressure, the stone is dry-set in the ancient fashion of cyclopean walls: large irregular rocks held in place by stone chips which have been inserted into the crevices.

The most puzzling aspect of this isolated native house was the barrel roof over the kitchen part. In a region without timber the centering of a vault must have posed almost insurmountable obstacles of wood supply. As it turned out, the Augustinians in the small town nearby kept a simple wood circe (Plate 61) in the church cellar which was loaned out to house builders in the hills. The vault itself was finished to excessive smoothness, rubbed down, as the woman of the place told, each year with the thorny stubble so abundant on the ground to eliminate all possible cracks, because this roof was the water shed of the dwelling. Each drop of the sparse precipitation and of the condensation moisture between hot day and cold night which rolled from the slick stone surface into rills on each side, was collected either in clay vessels or, in the best houses, in a small cistern. The heat of the sun warmed the massive stones during the day which were slow in giving up this heat to the sleeper in the interior at night. In all its bleak simplicity, this is a dwelling in which function and form coincide in rare totality.

61. DIAGRAM OF WOOD CIRCE

FORM AND FUNCTION: The Dwelling

62

127

KITCHEN HUT, EL TULE, OAXACA, MEXICO (64)

This is the cooking place of a modest Granja. It is eight by fourteen feet in size, with a fire pit, sunk into the tightly packed clay floor and an array of smooth clean stones for baking tortillas and grinding maize. The walls are twigs woven together by the sisal rope that keeps the horizontal bamboo poles in place. These twig walls are carried all the way to the ground and firmly planted into the sand to keep animals out of the kitchen interior. A kingpost on each gable end carries the ridge pole; above it is a legging of thatch to protect the jointure of the two roof slopes. Smoke, of course, escapes on all sides, but on the end near the fire pit, the twigs have been thinned out to allow quicker exit and keep the air inside the kitchen as clear as possible.

FORM AND FUNCTION: Working Space

When the European serfs deserted their feu-
dal lords and banded together in urban settlements, they soon discovered that they had to
expand vertically instead of horizontally to
accommodate all citizens within the protective
walls. The development of this structural
problem and its gradual solution can be traced
in the evolution of the medieval house wall
from the 13th to the 16th century. Half timber,
the most economic and the quickest building method, dominates the medieval town
throughout Europe, but the steadily rising
height of the gable wall posed a vexing problem of stability in a highly unstable construction method. The costly and space-consuming
buttress systems of the cathedral could not be
utilized, so the house builders experimented
with a solution that might have been suggested by the groined vault. They gave the
house façade a slight inward "fold" and reenforced the groin with a double timber framing.
The second story, being pulled in against the
massive stone base and the gable, acted as
brace (Plate 65).

The Iowa farmer who built this barn some
30 years ago was probably unfamiliar with the
experiments of European builders during the
Middle Ages, but he intuitively found a solution similar to theirs. Over his concrete base,
inclined inward, he raised a framed super-
structure flared outward, to meet at a point of
neutralized stress with the inward inclination
of the roof. The result is not only of great stability but of pleasure for the eye.

65. "FOLDED" GABLE, ÜBERLINGEN, GERMANY

FORM AND FUNCTION: Working Space

MENNONITE BARN, LANCASTER COUNTY, PENN-
SYLVANIA (69)

The next step in the development of the half
timber house in Europe was the framed overhang which allowed for almost limitless vertical expansion. As many as eight stories could
be raised above each other with the cantilevered floor joists carrying the corner posts of
the story above. A charming variation of the
overhang was the *Laubengang* (Plate 68) in
which the supporting posts of the second
story form an arcade together with the re-
cessed first story walls of the house. The Penn-

FORM AND FUNCTION: Working Space

68.  OVERHANG HOUSES, GERMANY, SHOWING "LAUBENGANG"

sylvania Dutch settlers were well acquainted with this framing method because they came from the south-west of Germany where whole towns are so constructed.

The Mennonite farmer who built this substantial barn around 1870 used the inherited knowledge for a different purpose. He wanted as much clear and unobstructed working space in the interior of his barn as he could possibly provide without weakening the barn structure. As a Mennonite he was bound to use only two building materials: stone and oak; all other materials were forbidden. He fashioned pilotis of fieldstone and hydraulic cement, tapering them in the exact angle in which the foundation wall of his barn spread outward (Plate 67). Then he laid a heavy oak beam across the piloti for the support of the cantilevered floor joists from the barn's second floor. Had he built a perpendicular wall in the usual manner, a portion of the joists would have been unsupported and therefore unstable, and the solidity of this second floor was of the greatest importance.

In contrast to English barns, the Pennsylvania Dutch farmer did not drive into his barn on the ground floor. He constructed a ramp in the rear of the building, driving his team to the loft from which the hay could be pitched down into the stalls and pens of the livestock whenever it was needed. It was this special handling of farm operations that gave rise to the unique form of the Pennsylvania barn.

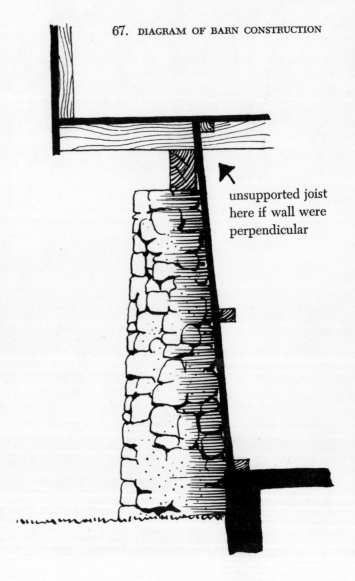

67. DIAGRAM OF BARN CONSTRUCTION

unsupported joist here if wall were perpendicular

FORM AND FUNCTION: Working Space

The Shaker sect of upstate New York offers one of the most curious examples of contrast in the American settler group. Mother Ann Lee, their leader, forbade private property, any form of adornment or ostentation, and all sexual relationship between men and women. Whatever she prevented her followers from doing, she certainly did not inhibit their technical inventiveness. These hermits in a rural wilderness invented the Turbine Water Wheel, the Circular Saw, a Fertilizing and Planing Mechanism, a Washing Machine, a Label Printing Press, and the Circular Barn. Perhaps it was the frustration of their celibate existence that spurred them to such originality. Whatever it was, there is not one of their numerous inventions that does not provide two advantages: economy of material and saving in human labor.

The massive stone barn from 1823 still stands today, but its huge front door has been so mauled by patchwork that it does not bear photographing. Its unique concept can, however, be understood from the rear view. In a square barn, either the team must be un-hitched to leave the building, or a second door must be provided at the opposite end, entailing severe loss in space and weather security. In the round barn, the team was driven along the curved interior, leaving by the same open-ing through which it had entered. A circular barn can be evenly lighted through a "lan-tern," here taking the form of a handsome turret which originally had louvres that moved with the wind to admit fresh air and daylight. A clearstory, gracefully constructed with twelve corners, provides additional light for the hayloft and the threshing floor. The diameter of the stone barn is 108 feet, telling of the prosperous economy of these strange unworldly technicians who could have conquered America with the inventiveness of their brains, had they not died out from lack of progeny.

FORM AND FUNCTION: Working Space

The round barn, first built by the Shakers, never became popular. Its obvious disadvantage is that it lacks loft space, since the roof rests on the walls thereby limiting span and height. In addition, there is no possibility of expansion, a hope that is dear to every American farmer. The advantages of circular construction are equally obvious, and they have again and again been tested by farmers in the mid-western states, but there is no other example of a massive stone barn, such as that of the Shakers. Later examples were built from wood to avoid the necessity of heavy timber framing. A circular building can be constructed on the principle of the barrel. Each row of vertical boards forms a hoop, held together by horizontal timbers which must be short and narrow. A barrel is stronger than a box and therefore more resistant to wind pressure. The University of Illinois, experimenting on its farm research station with circular barns, reported a saving of 22% in wall and foundation work, and 34% to 58% in building materials.

This Pennsylvania barn, however, is less impressive for its percentage-wise saving in materials and labor, than for its beauty of craftsmanship. It is covered with a wrap of split cedar shingles of such superb quality that it equals the finest carpentry one can find in oak framed houses. The roof is covered with the same shingles because they have a special advantage. Moisture, even a heavy moist fog, will swell the split wood and close the roof to absolute water tightness. During hot and sunny weather the shingles contract, letting air and light into the barn. The dairy room to the right has been joined to the round structure as a convenience, but it adds a formal counter point to the curve which is effective and pleasing.

FORM AND FUNCTION: Working Space

VILLAGE WELL, CHRISTIANSTED, ST. CROIX, VIRGIN
ISLANDS (72)

It might seem inconsistent to include a well
among examples of interior working space
achieved by adequate exterior form. This example derives its architectural importance from
the perfect spacing of its parts, its *coherence,*
which was mentioned in the introduction.
Spacing here is the function of the working
units, serving a continuous operation with
beautiful form. Steps, storage platform for the
receptacles, and the well itself are composed
as if an architect had conceived them and a
sculptor had moulded them. They are finished
in stucco of a delicate pink that gives a rose
glow in the strong island sun.

FORM AND FUNCTION: Working Space

STORAGE BINS, NOW FARMHAND HOUSES, ZACATE-
CAS, MEXICO (74)

As the Indians took possession of this continent, they kept the *brauch* of the tent they had
brought from the Asiatic steppe. It remained
the basic shelter type of their nomadic and
semi-nomadic existence, but the widely dif-
fering conditions of the habitat in the New
World enforced innumerable variations. The
conical bark hut of the Penobscot Indians of
Maine and New Brunswick (Plate 73), for instance, is far superior to the skin tīpi of the
Plains Indian although the basic construction
principle is the same. Snow and high wind
velocity had driven the northern Indians to
invent a continuously curved surface of a
double-layered covering that would shed snow
and rain.

In the Sierra Madre Range of Zacatecas,
some 4,000 miles further south, the climate is
similar to that of the Canadian seaboard, so
the Indians built for their Spanish masters
granaries resembling the Penobscot bark
houses, except that they were meant to be
permanent and burglary proof. They were of
stone, smoothly corbelled in the most ancient
and reliable stone construction method (see
Introduction, Plate 3) known to man. Square
steps to reach the ventilation hole are spared

out in the smooth surface, wrapped around
the conical shape with the flourish of a gar-
land.

Each of these structures is a perfect coordination of economy and durability. There is no
diversity. The variation of type, so basic to
all anonymous houses, is missing because these
were intended to be storage bins, not human
dwellings. Today the free but impoverished
farm laborers live in the stone huts as they
would in a city tenement, not knowing that
what they miss is the individual concept that
distinguishes animate and inanimate shelter
in anonymous architecture.

73. PENOBSCOT INDIAN BARK HUT

FORM AND FUNCTION: Storage

GRANARY, VALLEY OF OAXACA, MEXICO (75)
and CORN CRIB, NEW HAMPSHIRE (76)

Old people in New England call the tapered corn storage bin raised on wood blocks or brick an "Indian Crib." It is unlikely that the valiant but undomesticated northern Braves invented this effective construction that prevents rot in an easily perishable produce and supplies a continuous unobstructed flow from the wide top to the contracted base. The "Indian Crib," whose name was most probably derived from Indian Corn, exemplifies an interesting contrast in settler character. The dour, sober and basically unartistic English stock answers a specific need with a practical minimum structure. The inventive, form-conscious settlers of Spanish-Indian descent combine artistic form with desired function.

The small Mexican granary, six feet high, in a cactus field not far from Tehuitzinga arrests the attention because its superb, one might almost say sophisticated, composition stands out starkly against the desolation of this blaz-

ing wasteland. At one glance it becomes clear that the grain stored inside is of great value to the owner and that he has expended on this construction the same ingenuity and care which other people in other cultures expend on safes. A smooth earthenware urn is sunk into a stone base of dry-set pebbles and boulders. It tapers outward to prevent rodents from climbing up the side, but even if they did, they would find no hold on the tier of straw fringes, hemming the upper rim with the grace of a petticoat flange. Sun and the scarce rain are kept out by a hood of thatch and twigs, artfully interwoven, surmounted by a ventilation funnel of darkened wood. Apart from its efficient combination of purpose and construction, this little structure has such a distinct personality that it gives the impression of a whimsical child, evoking laughter and an immediate fondness for its grace and originality.

FORM AND FUNCTION: Storage

76

145

*Fortresses and churches are rarely built spontaneously. While the defensive site must be chosen according to specific circumstances (Plates 24 and 26), the construction of the fortification runs usually along traditional lines. The art of defense against assault by firearms has long turned into a science. This vital part of strategy is as universal as a religious dogma. The various fortresses built by the Spaniards in the south and the English in the north of the New World differ very little from each other and from the European post-Renaissance fortress. But every now and then the special circumstances of a newly settled area, and the isolation from centers of strategic planning, produced architectural forms of great spontaneity and intuitive intelligence.*

77

FORTIFIED GRANARY, PROBABLY 17TH CENTURY, TEOTYUCAN, MEXICO (77)

This might very well be the oldest existing example of a settler-built fortification. Its octagonal shape occurs in many Spanish defenses, showing Visigothic origin in contrast to the square Moorish towers. One of the earliest examples in the Western Hemisphere, the 16th century *El Rollo* (Plate 78) in Tepeaca, Puebla, looks like an educated version of the fortified granary. Both have in common the lack of openings, round-headed windows, and platform for lookout; but the granary, in contrast to the classical *El Rollo,* is pure vernacular. It has been stabilized by a unique adaptation of the medieval flying buttress. On very uneven ground, which threatened the foundations of a vertical structure, sixteen stone slabs follow the rise and fall of the site. They meet the wall at a high angle where the stress is greatest, namely at the corners, and at a low angle in the less imperiled center of the wall. The buttresses had another advantage; they left no space for the placing of ladders which were a major danger in the days of man-to-man assault. The fortified granary has remained sound for some 300 years in a region shaken by earthquakes, a monumental and beautiful form with an efficiently expressed purpose.

148

FORM AND FUNCTION: Defense

78.  EL ROLLO, TEPEACA, PUEBLA, MEXICO

149

The log-constructed blockhouse was the accepted mode of defense in the long struggle against both the Indians and the British Army. Most blockhouses are rectangular, based on the length of the timber. If they are round, they are usually paled, based on the vertical components of the palisade. The anonymous army engineer who constructed Edgecomb might have been inspired by the small octagonal Fort Erie built late in the 18th century, but he adjusted his structure to an exceptional site—a promontory on the Maine coast that was equally exposed to attack from the inland and from the sea. His octagonal fort allows a continuous observation of all approaches, and, most important, it gives to each opening total back protection from a structural core, from which twenty-four horizontal beams are cantilevered to carry the upper structure. A soldier backing away from an opening would not expose his back to an opening on the opposite side (Plate 79). He was protected by the central post.

The same static principle, mentioned in Plates 68 and 69, gives stability to this building that actually is an umbrella. Another deviation from standard log houses is the covering of wood shingle that sits with fine precision between the perfect joints of heavy oak framing. The bitter reality of man's fight against man, and the humanism of structure and materials, provide point and counter-point for a building which conveys more impressively than does the domestic scale "the sentiment of huge timbers" of which Whitman so lovingly speaks.

79.  DIAGRAM, FORT EDGECOMB CONSTRUCTION

**150**

FORM AND FUNCTION: Defense

Plate 24 showed the bold, one might even say mad, choice of location Henry Christophe made when he tried to realize his dream of a Citadelle to defend Negro independence. The interior of this vast structure is no less overpowering. Instead of the usual succession of casemates, magazines and galleries, here is a maze of enclosed battlefields, connected by arched openings of totally irregular height and size. The Citadelle had no glacis, no ramparts and parapets and no berm. All the fighting had to be done within its walls and there were no inaccessible corners. One sees soldiers like flying bats diving from the openings, driving the enemy mad in a labyrinth of interconnected spaces. There is another reason behind these arches of every conceivable width. There was no timber for lintels except shoddy palm trunks. The lay builders of King Henry's army labored for nine years to construct durable arches with the coarse brick they burnt from local clay. Not an opening has collapsed, not a wall caved in. *La Ferière* would have been invincible had it ever been put to the test.

The space shown in this plate is directly above the enormous underground cistern, scooped from the bare rock and connected with a network of wood gutters, directing every drop of water into the reservoir. 365 cannons, one for every day of the year, surrounded this hive of defensive spaces, planned to hold 10,000 soldiers in case of siege.

152

FORM AND FUNCTION: Defense

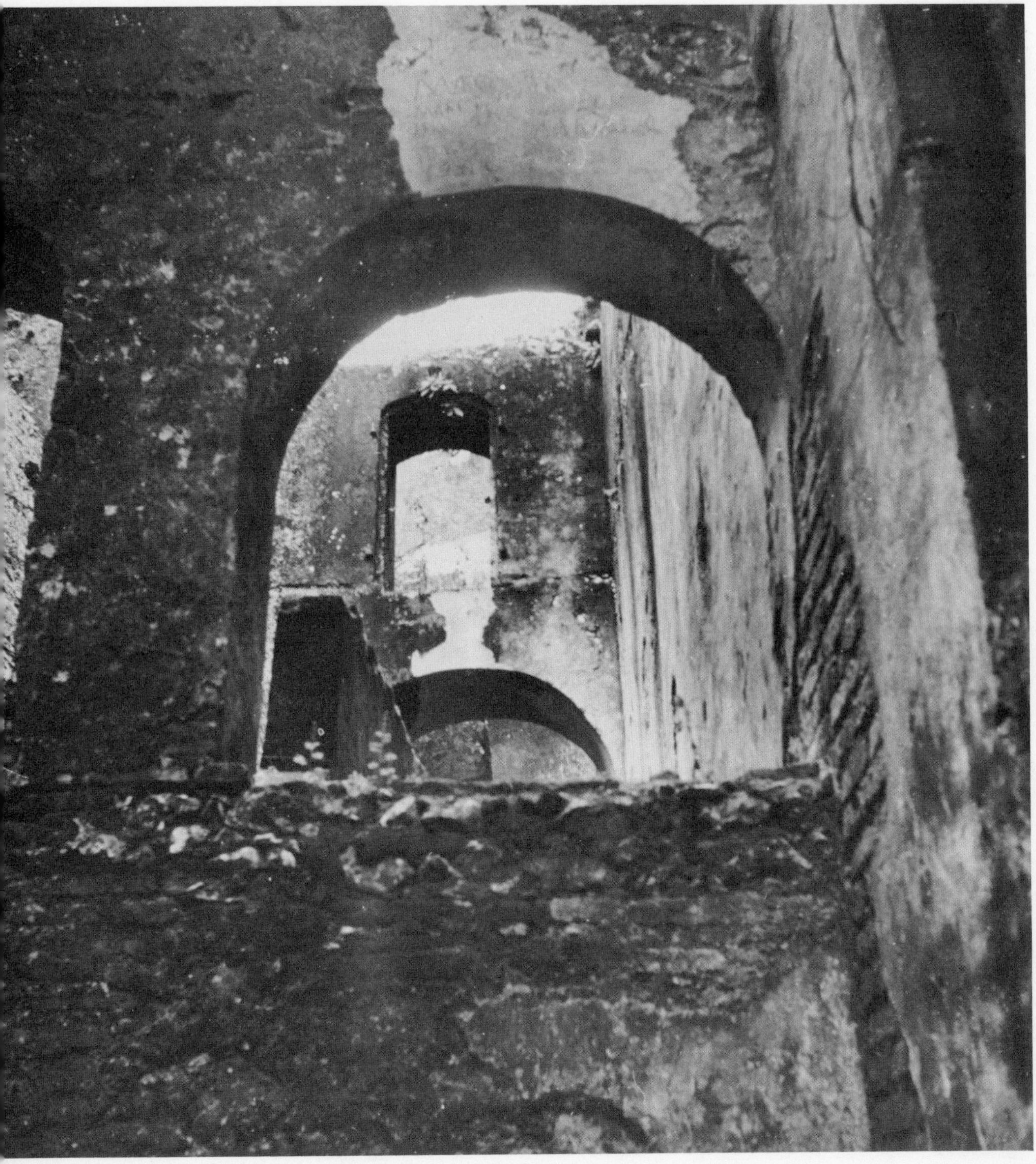

*The dogma of defense and the dogma of faith are abstractions that dictate the form of the structures that serve them. Again, as in the case of fortifications, the settler is occasionally so far removed from the centers of authority or so distinctive in his interpretation of doctrine that he achieves local variations and adaptations that are worth noting. The common denominator in church architecture is religious symbolism, signifying concerns outside the conquest of natural environment. The dwelling with all its ramifications of working, living and storing spaces, is image and not symbolism. If it is good, it is the image of man's sanctuary on this earth. By its structural and esthetic qualities it should depict the man within, like the work of a good artist who also must provide insights beyond the rendered form. The church is not image but symbol, the sign by which to know that man is in the keeping of God, a transcription of divine intentions into the material language of architecture. Plate 23 showed this symbolism expressed through the choice of the site; the four plates to follow express specific religious concepts, made architecturally interesting through unique adaptations to singular local conditions.*

FORTIFIED VILLAGE CHURCH, ILITA, PUEBLO, MEXICO (83)

"Ilita of the Spanish Tongue," as the bell-ringer called it, stands in modest challenge on a bluff, overlooking the dusty and rutted road that winds toward "Ilita of the Indian Tongue," lying unprotected in a jungle of maguey and cactus. The entrance with a small plaza is turned away from the road, the way the Protestant settlers of Pennsylvania had placed their cloisters (Plate 26). The massive form is symbol of both the challenge of the cross and the defense of those who follow it. The round tower which forms a curious, obliquely placed interior apsis, carries a roof of Spanish tiles, sitting on two oakbeams which are pushed through the solid masonry like two pins.

The interior ceiling, too dark to be photographed, is a strange and moving reminder of Spain's troubled past. The flat panels between adzed beams are covered with multicolored designs of unmistakably Moorish origin. These are the stylized flower and animal patterns of the ancient *alfarje* decorations which survive to this day in embroideries made in Granada, the heart of Moorish occupation 700 years ago (Plate 82). As symbols of the beauty of Creation, they delighted the semi-desert dwellers of North Africa who came to Spain, and they still delight the semi-desert dwellers of the arid Mexican plateau.

82. DIAGRAM, MOORISH EMBROIDERY AND CEILING DECORATION, ILITA

156

FORM AND FUNCTION: Worship

83

Exactly 300 years had passed since the death of St. Francis when the mendicant order of the Franciscans arrived in New Spain. The brotherhood of the poor, which the gentle Saint of Assisi had envisioned, had long since turned into a rigid organization with all the power and paraphernalia its founder had wanted to avoid. But there was to be one moment in history when St. Francis would have recognized the spirit that had possessed him. The first friars, sent by the powerful Spanish Church into the wilderness beyond the sea, were expendable. They were abysmally poor, ignorant of learning or luxuries, and deeply moved by love for the savages they had come to save. The unique element of dawning Humanism in the teaching of St. Francis, anticipating by several hundred years the Renaissance concept of Naturalism and man's concern with man, bore modest fruit in the first decades of Franciscan and Augustinian missionary work in Mexico. A generation later the good deeds of the humble Franciscan brothers were brutally and lastingly wiped out by the arrival of official representatives of the Spanish Church, but to this day there lives in the hearts of the Indios a tender memory of kindness and help which the men of the forlorn missions rendered to the forlorn natives.

In 1530 the Franciscans started a church at Xochimilco, near Mexico City. As was usual with them, they had to construct their edifice from local materials with local help and without the benefit of trained architectural advice. The great cathedrals of the Gothic past with ribbed vaults and stained glass windows were beyond their ability. All they could accomplish was the narrow low church of the Romanesque era, roofed by a simple stone barrel vault. In Xochimilco, which needed more than a chapel, they arrived at a touchingly naive and ingenious solution. They put what amounted to three barrel-vaulted chapels side by side, the way metal barracks are still constructed today.

In their first edifice they had neither the strength nor the material to build adequate buttressing. The only bracing they accomplished was highly original—heavy iron chains, extending below the vaults from wall to wall, but in 1580 the whole front of the church collapsed. This was by no means unusual. The lack of building skill among the mendicant monks took a heavy toll in lives and buildings. Perhaps it was as a result of this disaster that "flying buttresses"—not flying, but crouching like the backs of work elephants—were put against the crucial points where two barrel vaults met. The friars might have remembered the church of Santiago da Compostela or the massive buttresses of the old cathedral in Barcelona, but it is more likely that they shaped with their hands the stone bracing as it dictated itself from the point of greatest stress. The cupola over the intersection of nave and transept was joined to these invincible buttresses with a rampant arch that seems like a cable, connecting forces, in spite of its heavy form. The whole essence of the church at Xochimilco is strength—a strength of humility and endurance, expressed in indigenous architecture.

158

FORM AND FUNCTION: Worship

CHAPEL, ARMSTRONG PLANTATION, ST. CROIX,
VIRGIN ISLANDS (86)

Homesickness is the endemic disease of all
settlers. It accompanies the bold and practical
manifestations of a love for life and comfort
with an undertone of melancholia and lone-
liness. To the traveller, looking for recast
forms and concepts among the monuments of
rural builders, it often seems as if the heart-
break of the lost homeland were still linger-
ing in the alien air.

One of the Danish Governors of the West
Indies, a man of passionate temperament who
shared his many troubles with a beautiful
mulatto mistress, built this chapel in the second half of the 18th century. It is now almost
destroyed by earthquake and callous neglect,
but it still proudly retains a gable line of startling elegance. A rubble wall of coarse and
primitive construction is terminated by a superb arabesque of brick coursing, so well constructed that not one stone has fallen out of
place.

The "Knights of Malta" had held court on
St. Croix before the arrival of the Danes. Had
they left behind a Negro slave, trained in the
Baroque style? Did he translate the nostalgic
memory of his master, dreaming of Copenhagen's Christianborg Palace (Plate 85) and
its gabled roof? The musical line of the jungle-
choked chapel rings like the echo of a Bocche-
rini arpeggio.

85. DIAGRAM OF ONE GABLE AT CHRISTIANBORG
PALACE, COPENHAGEN, DENMARK

160

FORM AND FUNCTION: Worship

PRESBYTERIAN CHURCH AND PARSONAGE, NEW
MILFORD, CONNECTICUT (87)

The Meeting Houses of New England are as abstractly uniform as the Saltboxes. The arresting charm in this particular example comes from a physically and symbolically stated contrast to the parsonage. The men of Chartres, passing through the sculptured doorways of their cathedral, entered into the mystic transformation of the metaphysical Gothic faith. They expected to experience the Divine Presence in the monumental interior. The men of New England, passing through the white clarity of their porticoed halls, entered into the Protestant ideal of "a free association of free citizens, met without summons." The Greek Revival design of their church symbolized "testimony by scripture and reason alone." Its classical proportions were a rejection of 2,000 years of Catholic history. Beyond this religious symbolism there is in the noble simplicity of a Doric portico an esthetic appeal that defies the eclectic argument. Horatio Greenough, in spite of his revolutionary call for "form and function," could not refrain from saying: "I love to bear in my bosom a nosegay plucked in Classical ground. It sweetens me to myself."

The parsonage was outside this symbolism, whether spiritual or esthetic. It was a worldly affair, dedicated to service and well-being. There was no need to deviate from the standard house type that had developed from Puritan origins during the 18th century. Henry Hobson Richardson's Romanesque parish house in Boston, or the Neo-Gothic excesses on the secular additions to Upjohn's Grace Church in New York, would have made no sense to the Connecticut parishioners. To them, symbolism was the realm of the sacred district—the temenos of Neolithic days; reality was something else—a durable, economic and personal expression of man's human needs.

162

FORM AND FUNCTION: Worship

87

The inclusion of these monuments needs an explanation as does the village well in Plate 72. This, of course, is not architecture, meaning constructed shelter for man, beast, harvest, or for the idols of his religion, but there is a strange and compelling suggestion of the habitat of the dead here, expressed with a highly artistic originality. In a country beset by a poverty which seems almost beyond the imagination of an American, these heavy, permanently constructed sarcophagi are by no means confined to cemeteries. They often stand beside a family dwelling of such bareness and impermanence that it just manages to keep its inhabitants out of the weather.

Haitian peasants are unwilling to talk to white strangers about the actual meaning of these royal tombs for those who departed in want, but from various sources the architectural meaning could be inferred. The ancestor must be provided with a sumptuous dwelling to keep him near his descendants and, consequently, well-inclined toward their fate which he can make or destroy through his supernatural contacts. It is ancestor cult at its purest, no different in its architectural connotation from an Egyptian pyramid or a Shinto soul house. A typically Haitian feature is the extraordinary massiveness of these tombs. Not only can the ancestor not take flight, shirking on his protective duties, but also no voodoo charm cast by malice can penetrate this "castle." What actually prompts the tomb builder to arrive at a specific form, which is never duplicated, remains a mystery.

164

FORM AND FUNCTION: Worship

MATERIALS AND SKILLS  *part four*

Native building materials, taken from the environment of the settlement, have a resistance to calculated order which technological building materials do not have. Stone, clay, lime, wood must be handled according to innate properties that cannot be changed and must be accepted; such as stratification, grain, density, responses to load, temperature, moisture and aging. Good building depends on a familiarity with materials that comes with long observation, as if they were the character traits of a marriage partner.

The technological builder calculates weather and time as the most destructive forces acting on industrial building materials. Deterioration is the most important negative factor to be considered in the construction and evaluation of technological buildings. Native architects calculate weather and time as building aids. Time and climate are not liabilities but assets, working for and not against the builder. The blazing sun dries the adobe wall. The pouring rain hardens hydraulic cement. Force of gravity sets stone on stone. The aging of wood stops warping, and the absorption and evaporation of moisture make wood roofs "breathe" with the rhythm of the weather.

Building materials and methods were selected, not only under the aspect of *Werkgerechtigkeit* (adequacy to tooling and joining), but also under the aspect of *Zeitgerechtigkeit* (impact of time on matter).

The third factor in the selective process of anonymous architecture was *economy*. We think today of economy as the minimum provision at maximum profit, but the settler never thought of economic shortcuts. To be "economical" did not mean to save, but to prevent waste. A man might have to wait half a lifetime before he could build; but when he did, he used the best resources available. His concept of economy was that of the ancient house steward whose economy concerned the "oikos"—the household and not the cash balance. He managed the

89.   PAINTED BARN FRONT, ILE D'ORLÉANS, QUEBEC, CANADA

requirements and provisions of domesticity with respect for the human effort that had transformed the raw materials of nature into human sustenance. Economy in indigenous architecture means *maximum advantage* of all given factors.

Of all the concepts underlying anonymous building it is the specifically rural ideal of *quality* that is vanishing fastest. Cost and speed, the two driving forces of technological building, have affected rural building like a plague. The result is mongrel structures, half indigenous and half technological, that please no one and will not last. A barn on the Ile d'Orléans, Quebec (Plate 89), is a typical example. It still conforms to the old Canadian custom of painting barn walls and doors in vividly colored geometric patterns which have a double purpose. They indicate ownership, and they stand out in the heavy fog and drifting snow, making it easy to find the entrance. But the wall of this barn is covered with a stenciled tin sheathing simulating rusticated stone, surmounted by asbestos tar paper, simulating brick.

Good anonymous craftsmanship has certain characteristics that are constant, not only throughout the Americas but also in Europe. They are based on observation and *brauch*. Three wall details (Plates 90, 91, 92) may serve as examples for joining and finishing. They are from an 18th century well house in New Hope, Pennsylvania; a Huguenot House in New Paltz, New York; and a 15th century half-timber house on Lake Constance, Germany. Jointings, whether in wood or stone, are never concealed but rather emphasized. The wooden pegs or "tree nails" in half-timber structures acknowledge the "working" of green lumber. With each daubing of the infill, every ten years or so, the pegs are driven deeper into the wood to follow up the aging of the material. In stonework, binder is of great importance. It was the abundance or scarcity of lime that created characteristic regional construction patterns in the New World. Ashlar masonry is almost non-existent in vernacular building construction, but there is a wide variety of stone coursing. Stucco, as a finish, serves either as a cover for porous rubble or wattle and daub walls (Plate 57), or it acts as a heat deflector through whitewash (Plate 59).

90, 91. CORNERS OF WELL HOUSE, NEW HOPE, PENNA. AND HUGUENOT HOUSE, NEW PALTZ, N. Y.

The selective intelligence of the anonymous builder is another steady *Leitmotif*. He chose his materials under the double aspect of service and appearance, never giving preference to either but always combining both. Heavy materials and pronounced joints indicate maximum stress (Plate 97); lighter materials or lack of binder indicate stable areas (Plate 62). The combination of different materials, often employed in technological buildings for decorative effects, indicates in anonymous architecture a variety of functions and services (Plate 93). Even buildings of secondary importance show the marked intention of composition, a fusing into a harmonious entity by human craftsmanship and the mellowing of time. Anybody who has seen the meticulous reconstructions of bombed buildings in Europe must have been impressed with the hopeless inadequacy of new materials, lacking the intangible patina of the past. Anonymous buildings, if they are good, submit to aging as only the wisest of human beings can; they gather years as if they were fruit, not weight.

92.
CORNER OF MEDIEVAL HALF-TIMBER HOUSE WITH PEGS

93.
OHIO RIVER INN, LATE 18TH CENTURY, SHOWING SKILLFUL COMBINATION OF VARIOUS BUILDING MATERIALS

The priest in the valley church dated this wall from around 1600. It shows the ancient building technique of enceinte walls in European fortresses, in which local stone is piled on top of an earthmound enclosure. Here the old technique is adapted to particularly poor building material. The only available stone is the fieldstone (seen in the foreground), which seems badly suited to a wall of twenty-eight feet in height, particularly when this wall is amazingly slender, approximately three feet thick. But the settlers were not discouraged. They remembered the tower buttresses of Avila and Toledo which are recreated not only with absolutely firm knowledge of their static properties, but with an equally sure sense of proportion and spacing. They are heavily mortared where the outward stress is greatest, and they taper gracefully toward the upper rim where the bracing function is diminished. With the changing light of day, the undulation of the wall takes on a peculiar rhythm of looking convex from one angle and concave from the other. Of all the Mexican ruins this one is perhaps the most medieval in character.

WALL DETAIL OF AN OCTAGONAL COBBLESTONE HOUSE, MADISON, N. Y. (95)

The connection between the proud hacienda wall and this bourgeois mid-19th century dwelling is the brilliantly displayed ability to turn handicaps into building assets. The glaciers that covered the northern part of this continent left in their wake fields strewn with stones that range in size from egg-shaped pebbles to gigantic boulders. The Connecticut settlers cleared their fields by piling the glacial deposits into the typical stone walls that still separate Connecticut land holdings. In upstate New York the settler set his family to work collecting the considerably smaller prehistoric leftovers. Then he called in the local mason who built the usual "nogging" and daub wall which was the best he could do in a land short of timber and long on rubble. These walls were faced with a thick bed of mortar made with the abundant lime that was their advantage over the limeless Connecticut settlers. In this bed they set neatly coursed rows of cobblestones, inventing ever new combinations of colors and shapes, ranging from herringbone to eggcrate patterns. It was a laborious building process that had come from Europe where cobblestone houses are native to Southern Scandinavia. The result was walls of great durability that express the growing delight of the early Victorians in wall decoration without violating the unformulated principle of the entity of esthetic and structural function.

176

MATERIALS AND SKILLS: Stone

DOUBLE HOUSE, NEW HOPE, PENNSYLVANIA (96)

The English had their shipbuilding tradition which was transposed into the frame and board construction of New England. The Germans who came to Pennsylvania from the Palatinate were stone builders. Along the west bank of the Rhine, where building stone had been quarried since Roman times, stand the finest examples of European stone masonry in the three Imperial Cathedrals of Speyer, Worms and Mainz. This great heritage still echoes in the modest settler houses of Pennsylvania. Rural market towns like New Hope or Lititz have more fine wall construction than Boston or New York.

The twin walls, shown here, demonstrate the organic progress made in the course of a century in the selection of materials and the refinement of craftsmanship. The old part of the house dates from the first years of the 18th century. Its windows are set into the wall with a minimum of framing and are flush with the roof plate on the second floor to avoid "hanging masonry." The stones are neatly coursed to assure stability throughout. The new house from the end of the 18th century is joined to the old one with the same unselfconscious regard for old service and new demands that gives to Plate 56 a particular appeal.

Within a hundred years the simple settler had become the highly skilled craftsman. Stability now comes from the well-constructed quoins of sandstone boulders, set with a high degree of originality and intelligence. The stone infill requires less careful coursing than before because the wall is framed between quoins and a heavy footing of large dressed blocks. The rigid frame for industrial building was still more than a century away, but its principle is here completely understood. With lime being scarce, the binder is gypsum, forming a lively pattern on the dark red of the local stone like the veins standing out on a human hand.

178

MATERIALS AND SKILLS: Stone

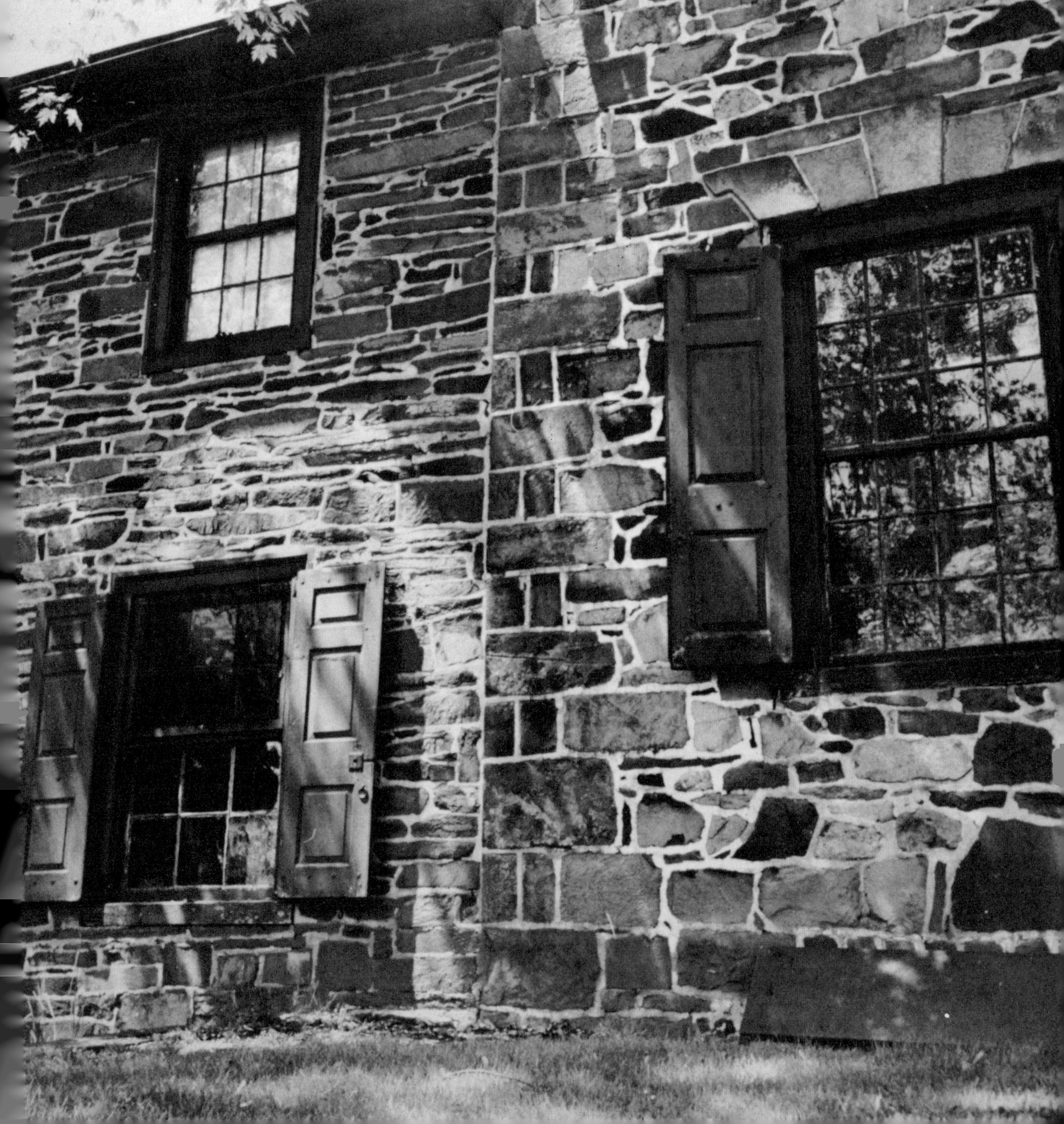

WINE STOREHOUSE, ST. THOMAS, VIRGIN ISLANDS
(97, 98)

This warehouse, and the arches forming the porch for unloading, were built by Italian workmen who came to the West Indies in the second half of the 19th century. What catches the eye at first glance is the rich color of the fieldstone, used in large units of bluish-grey, rust-red and brown as infill for the spandrels, the impost, and, in the interior, in small pebbles with many shades of blue, yellow, red and black. This is characteristic for all of St. Thomas where old plantation gatehouses in the hills often look like mosaic compositions, such is the beauty and coloring of their stone work.

At second sight it is the pure Roman heritage that startles in this structure. It would be difficult to find in Italy proper a finer example of the radiating brick arches, seen here, and of a wall that alternates in recreated *opus mixtum* brick and stone coursing. The echo of the Colosseum, of Rome's City Wall and of the aqueducts rings back from this structure of simple expediency.

**180**

MATERIALS AND SKILLS: Stone

"God made the other countries," is an old saying of the Dutch, "we made Holland ourselves." And it is not only the draining of the Polters they mean by that. Like the Mesopotamians they had to invent their own building material. The muddy soil of their homeland gave the raw material. Dutch ingenuity made it into the finest brick and brick workmanship known. The Pennsylvania Dutch settlers, called Dutch by a semantic blunder that could not distinguish between *deutsch* and *dutch*, adapted from their accidental namesakes the love for brickwork. Brick architecture is not native to the region of Europe from which they came. It was an assimilation from their neighbors, just as the overhang porch on Dutch houses, unknown in Holland, might be traced to the German "overshot" construction.

The brick-end barns of eastern Pennsylvania are a highly original variation of an adopted skill. Two types of brick are manufactured, both deviating from the Dutch standard size. One is much larger, measuring 2½ x 4½ x 9¼ inches, and the other is exactly half of these proportions. These two sizes are combined in open lacework patterns that are the first air-conditioning units of America. Perforation in solid walls equalizes air pressure between inside and outside. An even flow of air obtains that prevents the stored crops from rotting. The openings, small enough to keep rain out, but numerous enough to light the interior, are placed on the south wall against the weather.

It would have been normal to express a storage principle, based on almost scientific observation of storage and climate problems, in uniform patterns, but there are no two brick-end barns alike. It would have been as much of an offense to the Pennsylvania bricklayer to repeat the brick arrangement of his neighbor, as it was for the medieval carpenters to imitate each other's half-timber design. Both carry the individual signature of the master craftsman.

In 1676 a Dutchman, Wessel ten Brook, built his home in the upper Hudson Valley. He made the foundations from undressed fieldstone lumps and the walls from roughly dressed boulders, but for the Dutch Oven he used colored, glazed brick in yellow, red, pink and brown that delights the eye. The smooth half bell sits like an easter egg in the austere blackish-grey of the stone wall. The effect is highly decorative, and one might be tempted to think that this was the intention of the builder. This was not so at all. Glazed brick has a high heat-retaining quality. The Dutch Oven was the life-sustaining center of the kitchen. Here food was slowly cooked in a bed of hot charcoal ashes, heaped over the heavy iron kettle. The brick enclosure kept the heat alive long after the embers had died.

**182**

MATERIALS AND SKILLS: Brick

99

100

101

The Spanish conquerors had no scruples about adapting from the heathen Moors one of their most profitable skills: the making of glazed tile. Potters from Toledo, the center of Moorish life in Spain, came to Mexico in 1579, and from the 16th to the 18th century, the making of *azulejos* and the decoration of façades in the *mudejar* style were the main characteristics of Puebla—the City of Angels—and the province of that name.

It is from this earliest period that the patio enclosure in the small rural town of El Tepeaca dates. The tiles are still hand-shaped and hand-glazed. Their irregularity testifies to that, and so does the unfaded brilliance of the colors. All these tiles are blue—the blue of the sky from which the word *azulejo* is derived, and each tile has a different hue. The faint classical echo of the pilastered door jambs, the plain string course across the opening and the simple cornice are accentuated in their linear symmetry by the irregular tile mosaic that looks like the composition of a painter with a carefully balanced palette.

A hundred years later this intuitive craftsmanship had been replaced by factory methods. The "House of the Almond Cake" in Puebla from the last decade of the 17th century is typical Mexican Baroque. It has the controlled irregularity of the Chirriguresque architecture, but it lacks the compositional vivacity of the earlier tile work because every piece is uniformly colored and uniformly cut.

184

MATERIALS AND SKILLS: Brick

102

185

ENTRANCE TO SLAVE QUARTERS, ABANDONED
SUGAR PLANTATION, JAMAICA (103)

The slaves of the Babylonian Empire made a large, flat mud brick with convex sides, approximately 13 by 13 inches. The slaves of the British Empire, who certainly had never heard of Mesopotamia, produced bricks of very similar shape and proportion. They had to produce them for their own prisons which were dungeons tunnelled deep into the ground to make escape impossible. The only ventilation came from a narrow slot with an iron ringlet in the wall beside it where the occupant was chained down for the night. The binder for brick work in the West Indies was "mud and molasses" which had an excellent adhesion. Once it had set and dried, it could not be pried apart, but it attracted huge black ants that crawled over the brick walls and the slaves, and finally forced the use of lime or gypsum mortar.

The voussoirs forming the flat brick arch are almost a foot long and are set with a precision that is particularly astounding because there is no keystone. The enormous superincumbent load of earth and rock is evenly distributed to every element in the arch. This is a region of frequent earth tremors, but the slave builders knew how to construct their prisons to last for centuries.

186

MATERIALS AND SKILLS: Brick

Conrad Beissel, the prophet of the Anabaptists of America, was a remarkable man. In the best settler tradition he not only located his new homestead to provide the greatest advantage for his particular mode of life (Plate 26) but he devised, or at least inspired, a totally modern construction. The building is exceptionally high, having six stories. The whole structure consists of mortised oak beams, protruding over the interior studs by about six inches. They penetrate the "curtain wall" of clapboard and are protected by individual shingle coverings. The main beams, or "summers," have a span of 52 feet, supported every 8½ feet by a squared post. It is characteristic of the power of observation in these intuitive builders that the protrusion of the beams as a stabilizing method starts only at the base of the gable front where the brazing of the heavy corner posts ends.

The ceiling height in the interior is very low, around five feet, eight inches below the exposed beams. The reason was neither lack of long timber, as the summer beams show, nor a symbolic expression of humility, stressed by the five-foot door frames that made men bow low. The reason was Beissel's musical genius. He was not only a prolific poet whose "Songs of the lonely and abandoned Turtledove, meaning the Church of Christ" were printed in 1737 by Benjamin Franklin in Philadelphia; but he also was a composer of extraordinary talent.

Thomas Mann in his musical novel, *Dr. Faustus,* explains the architecture of Ephrata better than any historian could: "The music of Ephrata had been too unconventional, too strangely original to be accepted by the rest of the world. The voices had been aimed at the low ceiling of the Saal, and the listener had had the sensation as if the sound, unlike all known choral singing, had descended from there and had hovered, angelesquely, over the heads of the congregation."

MATERIALS AND SKILLS: Wood

ABANDONED WHOLESALE STORE, BAY CITY, MICH-
IGAN (106)

It would be interesting to find out who
brought the false gable to the Middle West
and Far West of North America. After the
demise of the Greek Revival, it suddenly turns
up in the baggage of the westward trains. Its
naively evident purpose is to pretend false
height and to serve as backdrop for ornamental detail. Naive? Indeed, but no more naive
than the Lombard gables of Pistoia, Pisa and
Pavia (Plate 105) that had served the same
purpose.

This old store, probably built around 1870,
distinguishes itself from thousands of its kind
by the astounding variety and loving precision
of carpentry work. There are five different
directions in which the clapboard siding has
been applied, and between each board there
is a neat piece of lathe to protect it against
warping and splitting. After many decades
without paint or maintenance of any kind, the
frames of the square, round, and pointed windows are still sound, and the frieze below the
cornice has lost none of its detail. Where today would the builder of a highway shack
think of lavishing so much imagination on
commonplace material, such care and precision on an entrance, set at a rakish angle into
the wall and followed with front steps of
diagonal cut? A building mattered—it was an
advertisement for the taste and quality of its
owners. With no radio and television commer-
cials, the impact of the store had to be "big as
life and twice as real."

105. DIAGRAM, FALSE GABLE OF LOMBARD CHURCH

**190**

MATERIALS AND SKILLS: Wood

The builders of this mill were of Dutch descent, but their work is a combination of many influences showing how by the year 1800 settler groups had merged. The large sails, once covered with canvas, are Dutch; but the smock type, in which only a mobile hood is turned into the wind instead of the whole structure, was an English invention. The octagonal plan differs from the prototype at Schermerhorn, Holland, by its considerable size. It is a logical layout, allowing for maximum space at the base where the grindstones are situated, and deflecting, by its tapering shape, as little wind power as possible from the sails.

An octagonal mill was also easier to frame for the exterior covering than a round one. This exterior covering was of split wood shingles, "cured" by submerging the wood for several weeks in a pool of salt water. The shakes, made by the family during the long winter evenings, were of amazing durability. On the Wyckoff house in Brooklyn (Plate 107) shingles cut in 1639 cover the south wall. They wore out at least three successive sets of nails whose iron proved less durable than the cured wood.

The shingle exterior is an ideal protection against rain and snow, and it is very American. Nowhere in western Europe could so fine a shingle exterior be found. One would have to go much farther north or east to the stave churches of Norway, or the mountain chapels in the Carpathians (Plate 108) where the native builder threw a shingle coat over the framing the way a peasant will wrap himself into an extra pelt in winter to keep his insides warm.

108. DRAWING OF CARPATHIAN MOUNTAIN CHAPEL

107. CLOSE-UP OF SHINGLES, WYCKOFF HOUSE, BROOKLYN, N. Y.

192

MATERIALS AND SKILLS: Wood

The two log houses shown here are a mere indication of the countless varieties existing in log construction. These examples are located at the northern and southern extremities of the North American continent, and they confirm the concept of economy common to all settler building regardless of location and ethnic origin. There is no date available for the New Mexico house. To judge from the large-sized panes of the double-hung windows, it must be at least 60 years old. The later mail-order variety has panes half that size. Even so the construction method dates back to the beginning of log cabin building in America, after the Swedes had brought their native building skills to Delaware at the end of the 17th century.

The tenon and mortise joints at the corner fit without nails and the caulking between the square hewn timbers is provided by the interior daubing of the walls. It is the downward pressure of the two-story structure that stabilizes the walls. The amazing aspect of this house, which dates it before the mill lumber days, is the adze marks on the beams. They show the characteristic cuts of an ancient spout adze which had a concave blade that left an imprint like the two fang marks of a snake. Split trunks are used for the framing of windows and door, indicating that mill lumber simply was not available to the builder. How handsome these round forms look against the flatness of the wall, an esthetic accent predicated by necessity!

Sometimes impermanence is as logical and organic for settler buildings as permanence (Plates 46 and 117 are further examples). The lumberjack leads a semi-nomadic existence. His shelter must be adapted to the cold of the North, made of easily available materials, and not constitute an encumberance. The Canadian woodsman is probably the only builder on earth who uses logs not horizontally or vertically, but who slices trees as if they were Bologna sausage. The chunks, eight or ten inches long, are set in a thick bed of gypsum to form a wall. Like the Eskimo igloo, this type of building can be erected in a day or two, because gypsum is the main deposit along the northern Atlantic seaboard, and cordwood is the byproduct of the saw mills. When the gypsum becomes brittle, usually after one hot summer, the walls grow porous; and when he can see the first sign of the sky through the cracks, then, the lumberjack says, it is time to move on to the next camp.

MATERIALS AND SKILLS: Wood

110

111

112. DIAGRAM OF TERRONE BRICK

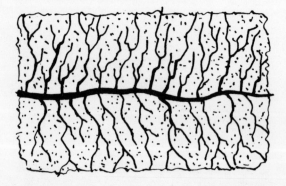

*Of all the adaptations of Old World building methods, adobe shows the most interesting variations in American settler architecture. It is an ancient Indian material fused with a construction skill native to the tribal settlements of Africa and Arabia. Before the Spanish conquest, the Pueblo Indians were predominantly stone builders. Their most original settlements, the cliff dwellings and Cavate*

lodges of Colorado and New Mexico, had masonry fronts and square or circular interior room divisions that showed perfect mastery of stone construction. When the Pueblo people left their cliff dwellings and moved into the valleys, they constructed their multiple "pueblos" not from stone but from a puddled clay mixture we now call adobe.

Prior to 1540, it was a very primitive construction method. The adobe mixture was dripped, course above dried course, until the desired height of a wall was reached, the way children build castles of sand that has been mixed with water. When the Moors conquered Spain in the 8th century, they brought across the Mediterranean some notable architectural achievements of Moslem-Saracenic culture: the masonry horse-shoe arch, arch stilts, squinched cupolas over octagons, and stalactite moulding.

Among the most humble imports of oriental brauch was the adobe brick. Since time immemorial it had been the native building material in the rimlands of the Sahara and Syrian deserts where sun and heat could be relied on to bake the clay mixture into stone-hardness. A wall of precast bricks was more handsome and above all more stable than a "drip" wall because the units could be coursed like kiln-burnt brick. This method of precasting adobe was introduced into New Mexico and Arizona by the Augustinian missionaries in the early 17th century. It was the most economical and the fastest way of building a mission and it was easily understood by the Indian workers who were familiar with the material.

There is one highly original variation from the standard Africo-Indian adobe block. It is confined to a single pueblo, Isleta, in New Mexico. This is Terrone, which is a square block of peat dug from the earth in four sharp cuts. A strong center root of the original bog plant forms the exact center of this natural brick, with the smaller side roots, extending from the center root, acting as reenforcements around which the clay-rich earth holds its shape (Plate 112). The principle is no different from the rod and wire reenforcements used today in concrete construction. The Mission of Isleta was built with Terrone and has needed no repairs since its consecration in 1672.

The usual adobe mixture consists of various concoctions of clay soil, sand, shredded grass, roots, straw, pot sherds and gravel, mixed with water and trampled by the feet of the builder into a soupy broth. Bricks vary from small 8 by 8 inches to huge adoberro blocks for wall structures which often measure 3 by 6 feet and are cast in heavy wood frames. The half dried brick is frequently "breaded" on the outside with ground sheep or cow dung which forms a protective layer. Each Indian community has its own adobe mix which is guarded as jealously as grandmother's cake recipe. The three following plates show three types of adobe construction to which many more variations could be added.

CHURCH AT TRAMPAS, NEW MEXICO (114)

VILLAGE WELL, LIBRES, MEXICO (115)

Of the three varieties of adobe work shown here, the poured adobe construction most closely resembles our modern concrete work. A "climbing" framework of boards is built first. Clay soil, mixed with straw and water, is poured between the shuttering. After the first pouring has dried, the framework is raised by nailing the boards higher to stakes driven into the ground. The process of pouring and drying is repeated.

The handsome angular design of the framed entrance door is reminiscent of the stylized patterns found in Peruvian blankets and pots. The interiors of mission buildings had fine wood ceilings (Plate 113). The lively accent came from the irregular outline of the stripped cross timbers which carried the flat roof, built up like a modern asbestos roof from many layers of poured adobe mix.

The same angular shape that is the natural result of climbing framework results from precast adobe blocks. They are joined with the smoothness of ashlar masonry and lightly plastered over with adobe mortar. This village well is particularly pleasing because of a carefully considered use of different materials and shapes. The deep well in the rear is used for human drinking water. It is shaded by a high wall of adoberros. The round well in the foreground is used to water the burros who stand head by head in a circle. It is built up from rubble and adobe mortar. The light red of its daubing contrasts most pleasantly with the warm yellow of the powerful rectangles in the background. The square outline against the sky, and the round hand-moulded ring below make a fine composition of harmonious form and specified function.

198

MATERIALS AND SKILLS: Adobe

114

115

199

One hesitates to say anything at all about this architectural still life for fear of making it banal. There should be a mere hint at the sureness of form-giving, at the obedience to function and the nature of materials. Although square, flat, pyramidal, oval and round forms are assembled in this very narrow field of vision, there is no disharmony, only harmonized contrast. The baking stoves are raised in successive rings like pre-wheel pottery, and then smoothed over with adobe mortar. One wants to reach out and feel the even roundness of the surface.

The Taos Indians who live here stand apart from the other Pueblo people. They are less bound by tribal clanship and they prefer a strong representation of laymen in their administration. They have no whipping ritual at initiation and no masked ceremonial dances. For as long as they can remember they have intermarried with Plains Indians. This progressive independent streak in their character made them call in their Mexican neighbors when they were hard-pressed by Apache attacks. From the Mexicans they adopted wheat-growing and the grinding of flour between stones. With this new diet came the round baking stove, three to six feet in diameter, a non-indigenous structure, created with the ancient technique of the hand-shaped mud-clay form.

200

MATERIALS AND SKILLS: Adobe

SUMMER BOWER AROUND HAITIAN HOUSE (117)

The last example of the unity of material and skill, with its accompanying accents of economy and diversity, is constructed of the most impermanent of all building materials: stems and leaves. Yet it is so structural, so functional and so pleasant that it deserves to be recorded. Away from the cooling sea breeze, summers in the West Indies are ferocious. All architecture in this area is geared to one aim: to catch the cool night air that will make sleep possible (Plates 40, 44, 58). The enormous diversity of solutions has been pointed out before.

Here palm branches are stuck into the ground at measured intervals. Their leaves are artfully interwoven to form a continuous enclosure strengthened in the center of each mat wall by a palm trunk that is joined to the main beam of the matted roof. This roof of loosely laid palm leaves is dense enough to give shade, yet porous enough to let the rising heat escape. Here the family lives and sleeps during the hot months, sheltered within their own walls yet capable of observing all that passes on the outside which is of great importance to the people of Haiti who are exceptionally companionable.

202

MATERIALS AND SKILLS: Fibre

# A SENSE OF QUALITY *part five*

Architecture is a form-giving art. Its impact on man comes from the interrelationship of enclosing walls and shaped interior void. This is a highly personal experience for the inhabitant, based on all the intangible factors of individuality. There are no universally applicable standards for the distribution of mass and space. Each plan is good which satisfies the physical and psychological needs of the dweller.

But there is another aspect to form-giving through architecture that is more universal. Buildings are the predominant accents on the human landscape. They influence the judgment of proportion and form of those who live among them because it is by the solids that surround us that we acquire our three dimensional perception. Ever since man came of age with the Industrial Revolution and granted to each individual the right to judge and be judged on relative, non-collective terms, this three dimensional perception has lost absolute qualitative standards. We no longer know what is good or bad in architecture, but an alert and interested individual has "a certain feeling" about what he sees. An instinctive response reacts to quality in form. It was once suggested that this innate sense of quality in architecture could best be exercised by evaluating four features of a house, and finding in them a certain measure for the success or failure of the builder's intentions.

These four features were specified as: the roof, the corner, the base and the access. The concluding plates of this book will bring two examples each of these features, chosen for their harmony in materials, composition and purpose. There will be no further commentary because it is hoped that through the preceding pages the reader has acquired a judgment of his own and can detect and enjoy the significance of the sheltering roof, the profile-giving corner, the anchoring base and the signature of the door, in the anonymous architecture of the New World.

118. GRANJA LINDA NEAR TULANCINGO, HIDALGO, MEXICO

THE ROOF

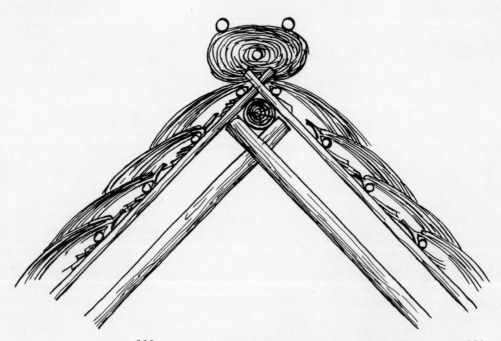

119.   DIAGRAM, CONSTRUCTION OF THATCHED ROOF IN PLATE 120

210

THE ROOF

120.   MESTIZZO HOUSE, MAYA REGION, CHIAPAS, MEXICO

211

121.  HOUSE IN CAJON CONSTRUCTION OF A NAVAJO SHEPHERD, ARIZONA

212

THE CORNER

122.  WOOD QUOINS OF A TENANT HOUSE FROM 1887,  MOHAWK VALLEY, N. Y.

123.   THE WILSON POPENOE HOUSE, ANTIGUA, GUATEMALA

214

THE BASE

124. CIRCULAR MANOR OF ABANDONED PLANTATION NEAR CHRISTIANSTED, ST. CROIX, VIRGIN ISLANDS

125.   DIVIDED DUTCH DOOR, VAN DEUSEN HOUSE FROM 1723, HURLEY, N. Y.

ACCESS

126.   GATE IN THE ADOBE WALL OF THE OLD TOWN, ALBUQUERQUE, NEW MEXICO

ACCESS

## AUTHOR'S NOTE

Research and photography for this book
were made possible by a grant from
The Arnold W. Brunner Fund
awarded to the author by
The Architectural League of New York

## CREDITS

Line Drawings by ROBERT FLEURY

HERBERT BAYER: Plate 35
MAJA DEREN: Plate 44
LAURA GILPIN: Plate 59
EARL LEAF (Rapho-Guillumette): Plate 42
LIBRARY OF CONGRESS COLLECTION: Plates 6, 15, 20, 22, 23, 34, 36, 38, 39, 66, 71, 93, 106, 110, 113, 114, 123, 126

GABRIEL G. MAROTO: Plates 47, 74
JORGE OLVERRO: Plates 7, 120
JAN ROWAN: Plates 116, 121

All other photographs by the author

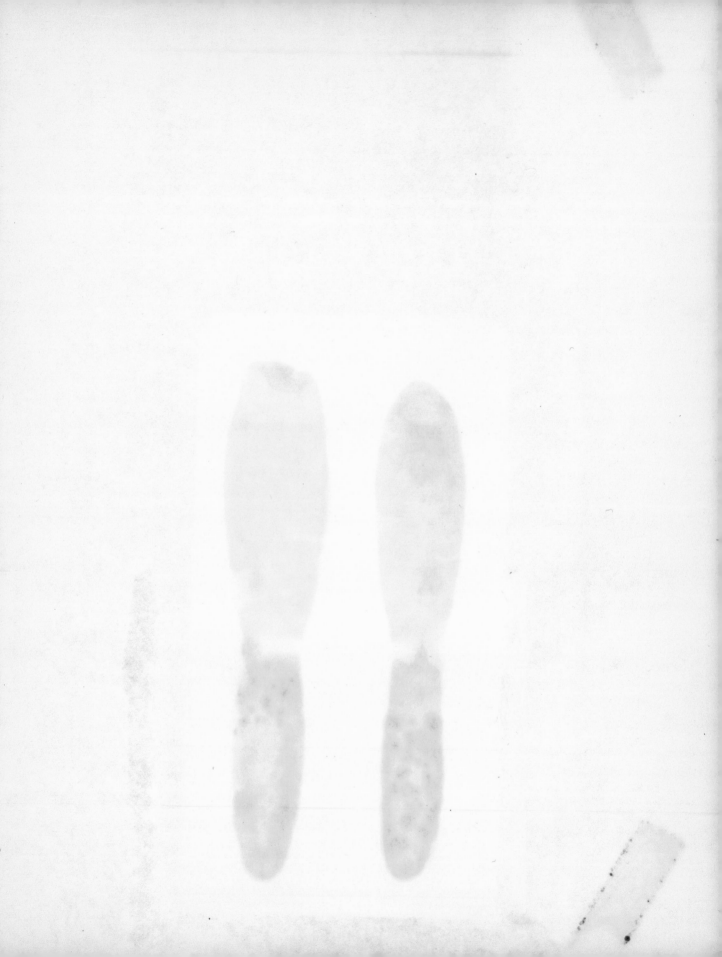

| DATE DUE | |
|---|---|
|  |  |
|  |  |
|  |  |
|  |  |
|  |  |
|  |  |
|  |  |
|  |  |
|  |  |
|  |  |
|  |  |
|  |  |
|  |  |
|  |  |
|  |  |
|  |  |

GAYLORD                                    PRINTED IN U.S.A.